TURKEY
AN AERIAL PORTRAIT

FOLLOWING PAGES:
A large part of the city's traffic on both sides of the Golden Horn
and the Bosphorus is provided by boats. The passenger ferry
shown here is passing in front of Haydarpaşa dock at the
Anatolia railway terminus on the former Baghdad line.

Text by Stéphane Yerasimos translated from the French
by William Snow
Edited by Emily Emerson Le Moing
Editorial Coordination: Emmanuelle Laudon
Designed by Louise Brody

LIBRARY OF CONGRESS CATALOGING-IN-PUBLICATION DATA
Rossi, Guido Alberto, 1949–
Turkey : an aerial portrait / photographs by Guido Alberto Rossi ;
text by Murat Belge and Stéphane Yerasimos.
p.   cm.
Includes bibliographical references (p.   ) and index.
ISBN 0–8109–3866–9
1. Turkey—Pictorial works.   2. Turkey—Aerial photographs.
I. Belge, Murat.   II. Yerasimos, Stéphane, 1942–   . III. Title.
DR417.2.R67   1994
914.961'0022'2—dc20   93–31352

Published in 1994 by Harry N. Abrams, Incorporated, New York
A Times Mirror Company

Printed and bound in Italy

TURKEY

AN AERIAL PORTRAIT

PHOTOGRAPHS BY GUIDO ALBERTO ROSSI

ORHAN DURGUT AND ARA GÜLER

TEXT BY MURAT BELGE AND STÉPHANE YERASIMOS

HARRY N. ABRAMS, INC., PUBLISHERS

CONTENTS

The high plateau reaches an altitude of 2,000 metres (6,500 ft.) in the east of the country, and is interspersed with mountains rising to 5,000 metres (16,300 ft.); agriculture becomes increasingly impractical at the higher altitudes. Shown here, flat fields below and terraced cultivation higher up.
PAGES 6-7: Haghia Sophia in Istanbul. In the foreground, the sultans' mausoleums and behind them the church of St. Irene within Topkapı Palace's first courtyard. In the background, the entrance to the Golden Horn, and on its banks the basket weavers' pavilion, one of the palace's outbuildings.
PAGES 8-9: The mosque and ruins of Ilyas Bey's *medrese* (college) at Balat, formerly Miletus, which became the capital of a Turkic principality in the 14th century. Ilyas Bey, its last ruler, had this mosque complex built near the ancient theatre in 1404.
PAGES 10-11: A path between two fields on the Anatolian plateau, used mainly by a village's flock of goats and sheep.

When Constantine the Great chose to change Byzantium's name to Constantinople and make it the capital of his Eastern Roman Empire, the golden milestone was erected in the centre of the city where the Imperial Palace and the Haghia Sophia (Aya Sofia) were to be built, and this was considered to be the centre of the world. When one visits Turkey today, one feels the Romans were not far wrong: nowhere else seems such a melting pot of peoples and cultures, such a pronounced link between East and West. The geography of the country is equally diverse. Turkey, partly in Europe and partly in Asia Minor, has a long coastline along the Black Sea in the north, the Aegean in the west and the Mediterranean in the south, and each of these bodies of water is quite different from the others. High mountain ranges run parallel to the sea in the north and in the south, leaving a vast plateau in the middle.

The eastern part of Turkey is very mountainous. To cross from any one of these regions into another is like entering a new world. The passage from the deep green of Turkey's coastline into its arid interior, to an other-worldly landscape like Cappadocia's, with its weird volcanic outcrops known as "fairy chimneys", is like going from a gallery full of rich oil paintings into one where only pencil drawings are displayed: nature in Turkey is always surprising. The bare steppes have only a short period of green in the spring, but sunrise is always beautiful there. The white slopes of Pamukkale, the ragged peaks of the Taurus mountains, the lake district in the southwest, the labyrinthine delta at Dalyan, and the amazing canyons in Antalya are all very different, and all very beautiful. But it is not only Turkey's natural beauty that is stunning. Everywhere, one encounters vestiges of the past, remnants of this or that people who at one time made the country their home. Near the resort of Dalyan are found the remains of the ancient Lycian city of Caunos. Not far from the warm pools of Pamukkale, where the swimming is delightful, lies ancient Hierapolis.

Turkey has always been a crossroads in Asia Minor. Continents and their topography impose certain itineraries, almost like the force of gravity. Mountains, valleys and rivers beckon people to move in a certain direction, which in time becomes an established route; Turkey is criss-crossed with such ancient pathways. But the country has always been a cultural crossroads as well, as each successive ruling civilization made its mark on local customs, and borrowed from these customs in return. During and after the Greek invasion of Asia Minor, many local goddesses of the agrarian communities were transformed, in Greek mythology, into fair young maidens ravished by Zeus, a metaphoric explanation for the various sorts of cultural assimilation taking place. The origins of much of Turkey's folklore are lost in time. For example, a certain folk-saint, Telli Baba, whose tomb is in Sarıyer, a village on the European side of the Bosphorus close to the Black Sea, is believed to help young girls to find husbands for themselves. Although there are officially no saints in Islam, Telli Baba may be the Moslem adaptation of an earlier Christian saint, perhaps a woman, who provided such a service. But then, who can tell whether that Christian saint had his or her origins in an earlier, pagan figure? In Turkey, the past is a rich labyrinth.

ANTIQUITY ■ We know that Anatolia was inhabited from very early times. In the Karain cave near Antalya, excavations have revealed remains of a settlement from the early palaeolithic age, and it has been deduced from the study of certain

Old maps lack the accurate detail of an aerial photograph, but have their own charms. In this example, the Golden Horn looks wider than the Bosphorus; clearly, achieving a pleasing composition was deemed more important than topographic accuracy by the map's creator, Matrakçi Nasuh, in the 16th century. Nasuh was a man of many talents: a fighter, mathematician, historian, and calligrapher, but above all, a miniaturist, as one can judge by this map. He made similar maps for many towns, which are invaluable today because in these he chose to try to show buildings as they really were.

skulls that Neanderthal Man was also a resident of Asia Minor around 140,000 years ago. But the oldest remains of what we can classify as a "civilization" found in Turkey belong to the Hatti, followed by the Hittites. The Hittites, an Indo-European people, reigned here from the beginning of the second millennium to the 8th century BC. Compared to the Karain cave, this is contemporary history. They were in contact with the Assyrians, often trading with them but warring with them as well. The Hittites probably borrowed their cuneiform alphabet from the Assyrians, as well as many Mesopotamian religious beliefs. This merging of cults continued in the Greek period, when, for instance, the Mesopotamian Tammuz became the Greek Adonis.

GRECO-ROMAN ANATOLIA ■ The Greeks arrived in Turkey in successive waves and gradually merged with the local population. The political system the Greeks brought to Turkey was one based on independent cities, and cities are still of primary importance in this region. When cities became overcrowded, part of the population set sail for a suitable site to establish a new colony, modelled in its customs on the mother-city. It was for this reason that the Phocaeans emigrated west to found the colony of Massalia (modern Marseille). The flourishing Mediterranean cities were the birthplace of a highly sophisticated civilization. Two agricultural discoveries of prime importance came into being in this culture : olive oil and wine, around both of which cults were formed. Alexander's empire was vast but relatively short-lived. It lasted long enough, however, to spread Hellenistic culture throughout what would become Turkey, because Greece's political and military expansion initiated a tremendous network of commodity exchange – a force that worked for uniformity on many levels. The Roman contribution to Turkey's development was very similar, though on a larger scale and ultimately more long-lasting.

During the period of the Pax Romana, a new invasion of Anatolia from the south-east began. This was not a military invasion, but rather a spiritual one. St. Paul, St. John and many other prominent Christian leaders were active in Anatolia in the 1st century AD, spreading the teachings of Christ, conquering not land but the hearts of men and women. Similar activities were taking place in the West, including in Rome, the heart of the Empire. Thus, Christianity conquered the mighty empire from within, and in the first half of the 4th century, Constantine the Great made it the official religion. At the same time, Rome was no longer strong enough to maintain peace and order throughout the vast domain nominally under her rule, nor to establish effective protection of her borders against ceaseless barbarian raids. Constantine decided to divide the empire into two parts.

The East needed a new capital. Constantine first thought of rebuilding Troy, no doubt with its historical importance in mind, but then chose Byzantium instead. He must have preferred the future that this city promised to the past that Troy represented. It was a wise decision. Constantinople became a thriving city, a real metropolis, very quickly, and

Mount Ararat is regularly visited by people determined to find the biblical Noah's Ark (Moslems believe the ark landed on Mount Cudi). There is historical evidence to encourage such exploration, although all traces of the Ark itself have disappeared.

Another early map, this one more accurate. We can see major monuments (Haghia Sophia, the Hippodrome, the Golden Gate) more or less in their correct positions. The map also reflects early Ottoman culture, thus it is a map of Istanbul in transition. The Mese, the main avenue that extends from near Haghia Sophia towards the city walls, is clearly shown.

Until the 18th century, the Bosphorus was edged with small villages scattered along the shore like beads on a string, without any connection to Istanbul other than by boat. The villagers lived by fishing or by cultivating fruits and vegetables. When the Ottomans came to the end of their military expansion, the sultans began to grant land along the Bosphorus to prominent families. After the introduction of the steamship in the 19th century, settlement was rapid and widespread. Both views are seen from the European side, almost from the same point, near the Black Sea. The fort in illustration (top) was built after a raid by Cossack pirates in 1624. The "Genoese castle" (bottom) was actually built by the Byzantines and taken over by the Genoese only when the great empire had been reduced to a single city. The high peak behind the fortress is where Yuşa, or Joshua, lies in the Giant's Cave.

sustained this role for a long time. There were many reasons that such an East/West division seemed appropriate, and once the division was formally made, everything began to emphasize it. Among the many factors involved, one was certainly religion – eastern and western Christianity were to develop, from then on, along separate lines.

When did the Eastern Roman Empire turn into the Byzantine Empire? This has always been a problematic question, and one reason is that the Byzantines never thought of themselves as anything but the heirs of the

A rather imaginary "map" of Constantinople, probably not drawn from direct observation. This is probably an attempt to depict the Imperial Palace and the Hippodrome.

Roman Empire. Justinian was the last emperor who might have been expected to reunite the Roman Empire. During his reign (527-565), an artistic renaissance went hand-in-hand with material prosperity, culminating, for instance, in the building of Haghia Sophia. Justinian also sent his troops to Italy and Northern Africa, and the Byzantine presence in Ravenna lasted for some time.

In William Butler Yeats's poem "Sailing to Byzantium", the poet complains of old age, which is such a contrast to "the mackerel-crowded seas" where "fish, flesh, or fowl, commend all summer long / Whatever is begotten, born, and dies". Yeats wants to reach a land where he can find "sages standing in god's holy fire". He says, "And therefore I have sailed the seas and come / To the holy city of Byzantium". Perhaps it was fortunate that this voyage of Yeats was only a poetic one, because he might have been quite disappointed by reality. What if he had arrived during the time of the Empress Theodora, who had a house of repentance built along the Bosphorus for prostitutes, and who was totally unrepentent concerning her own sins? And how would Yeats have felt if he had arrived during the turbulent "Scandal of Tetragany", Emperor Leo's attempt to legitimize his bastard son? The holy city was not always holy, after all. But the Byzantine Empire did produce magnificent architecture, literature, music and scholarship - and even poetry. A lot of sincere piety accompanied the highly publicized vices of Byzantium's Emperors and Empresses, and the monastic life had many adherents. But political machinations were so widespread and so often violent here that they gave rise to the expression "Byzantine intrigue".

ISLAM AND THE TURKS ■ After the 6th century, a fresh danger began to threaten the Empire. A new monotheistic religion, Islam, born in the Arabian peninsula, not far from the birthplace of Christianity, was brought to the empire by Arabs trying to establish their own empires. Not long after the death of the Prophet Mohammed, Arab armies began to besiege Constantinople. But though this Moslem menace was considerable, it was not powerful enough to overcome the Byzantines, probably because Islam found easier acceptance among other Arab and related peoples from North Africa all the way to Spain. Thus, Arabs eventually turned their attentions elsewhere, but Byzantium was next threatened by a new wave of invaders from the East: the Turks. The Seljuks were the first of these to arrive. Their first state had been established in Iran, but after the

The Galata bridge, built in the second half of the 19th century, and the earlier Unkapani bridge, were important factors in the modernization and urbanization of the city, as they connected the two shores of the Golden Horn and thus unified Istanbul.

battle of Malazgirt in 1071 (five years after the Norman invasion of Britain), where they defeated the army of Diogenes, they moved into Anatolia and pushed the Byzantines further and further back towards the western tip of the peninsula. They re-established central authority and restored control over the trade routes. Control of the silk and spice trades was actually the main source of income for the Seljuks, and this is reflected in the architectural works that remain from those times. Superb caravanserais were their original architectural contribution.

THE OTTOMANS ■ It was the inevitable internal decay of the Byzantine Empire that brought another Turkish dynasty, the Osmanlis (Ottomans), to the fore. Several small Turkish states had succeeded Seljuk rule in Anatolia after the onset of the Moghuls. Among them were the Ottomans, an Oguz-Tukmen tribe who had arrived relatively late to what is now Turkey. Nature abhors a vacuum, and so does history. As the Byzantine Empire disintegrated, the Ottoman Empire expanded. By this time, Anatolia had become overpopulated. The only solution was for some people to emigrate to the more fertile lands along the Balkan coast, which is what the Ottomans chose to do. In about 250 years, this small nomadic tribe had gone from strength to strength to become the vast empire of Süleyman the Magnificent. The Ottomans made their own contribution to the ongoing synthesis between the beliefs of the Turks and of the Moslems. Islamic ideology is ambivalent concerning conflicts between two sets of religious beliefs. Islam favours *jihad*, or the idea of religious conquest, by force if need be. But on the other hand, one can see examples of exactly the opposite kind of behaviour in the history of Islam. When Mohammed came to Medina in 622, he signed an agreement with the native Jewish community there, as well as with other "non-believers", in which he demanded their political obedience but left them free in their religious observance and the conduct of their internal affairs. The Turks applied the latter method as a rule; not coincidentally, in an Islamic state, the Moslem population was exempt from many taxes which non-Moslems had to pay, so it was more prudent to have a lot of tax-paying infidels rather than a homogeneous society of non-paying believers.

Mehmet II, known as *Fatih* (the Conqueror) because of his conquest of Constantinople, considered himself, as had others, to be the heir of the Roman Empire. He made his first serious agreement with the Greek community, appointing Gennadios (one Orthodox prelate who preferred the "Islamic turban" to the "Catholic tiara") to the post of Ecumenic Patriarch of the Orthodox Church. He then invited the Armenian bishop of Bursa to become the Patriarch of Istanbul, allowing groups of Armenians to settle in Constantinople for the first time. Mehmet II's son, Beyazıt II, invited the Sephardic Jews suffering at the hands of the Spanish Inquisition to live in the capital and in other parts of the Ottoman Empire. In this way, the multi-ethnic, multi-religious and multi-cultural *millet* (nationalities) system of Ottoman society gradually came into being and endured without major problems until the 19th century, the so-called Age of Nationalism. The

Turkish-Moslem civilization that the Ottomans created was neither Turkish nor Moslem, but Ottoman; that is, it was designed to ensure that all citizens of the empire, no matter what their ethnic backgrounds, would become loyal servants of the state.

WESTERNIZATION ■ Ottoman expansion stopped in the 16th century, after the failure of the siege of Vienna. This was a profound reversal of fortune. The East had always been powerful, unified and stable. The West, by contrast, had been riven by constant struggles of every possible kind. In spite of the West's upheavals, however, its civilization advanced so rapidly that, especially after the 19th century, the East was clearly the weaker of the two. And the apparent timelessness of the Ottomans proved to be stagnation and incompetence. The West colonized the Ottoman world economically. The non-Moslem sectors of Ottoman society were more prepared for co-operation with Western traders: their religion was closer to the West's, they usually learned western languages easily, and their exclusion, as non-Moslems, from the Ottoman Empire's political élite encouraged them to use economic means to better their position in society. Ottoman *pashas*, though still seeming omnipotent, began to rely more and more on Levantine, Greek or Jewish bankers, money-lenders and merchants. In a society where industrial production was still very limited, finance and merchant capital became predominant. All this took place in a context in which rising nationalism was shaking the foundations of Ottoman unity as nation after nation won the struggle for independence. The Ottoman Empire, besieged from without as well as from within, finally ceased to exist, to all intents and purposes, at the end of World War I, and out of its ashes rose the Turkish Republic.

ISTANBUL ■ Istanbul is still a beautiful city, typically Mediterranean in some ways but with a very distinct character of its own. What makes the city unique, loved by so many? Just as Rome was built on seven hills, Istanbul lies at the meeting point of two seas, the Black Sea and the Mediterranean, giving the city a key strategic position along ancient trade routes. East and West meet here: the straits of the Bosphorus and the Dardanelles divide Asia and Europe. Istanbul's Golden Horn, a perfect natural harbour, has always given it an added advantage. And a major factor in the city's greatness has always been the diverse groups of people who have settled in this international crossroads, contributing to the city's colourful culture.

This great city has withstood many threats over the centuries, but of all these, the 20th century rush to "modernize" may prove to be the most destructive. Many groups of people who once contributed to Istanbul's local colour are no longer to be found in the city, and many fine landmarks have been destroyed, particularly during the early period of the Turkish Republic with its official commitment to Westernization. But the richness of Istanbul's past is such that it is surviving even the menace of modernity, and the city still inspires fascination and even love among visitors and residents alike for its superb natural setting, its many remaining historic landmarks, and, most of all, for its lively population.

After the building of the Galata bridge, the main arteries of the city became those on a north-south axis instead of the ones on an east-west axis which had been dominant in the past.

No 94. Vue de Foundoukli, et Dolma-Bagtche

Dolmabahçe Palace and Mosque as seen from Galata, with the newer Çirağan Palace, now a hotel, in the background. In geographical terms, the new palaces are situated to the north of Topkapı, but the cultural direction of the move was felt to be westward. BOTTOM: The meeting point of the waterways seen from the fire tower of Beyazıt, in the old city. In the middle is the the Valide Han, the biggest caravanserai of the city. Since it was near the harbour, trade and manufacturing were concentrated here.

The Golden Horn seen from the old city (TOP). The Galata Tower, wearing its cap, is prominent on the other side. The mosque by the water was built in 1550 by Sinan for Rüstem Paşa, Süleyman's grand vizir, and is one of the city's most exquisite. BOTTOM: Seen from the Galata Tower, the Nuruosmaniye mosque (1755), the Blue Mosque (1617) and the Atik Ali Paşa mosque (1496). In the foreground are the domed roofs of the two bedestens of the Grand Bazaar. The large building on the left is the old Parliament building, destroyed in a fire. FOLLOWING PAGES: View from the Galata tower of the old city: the Seraglio Point, Haghia Sophia and the Blue Mosque.

de la Pointe du Serail. N: 192.

LAND OF CONTRASTS

Turkey is a land of many contrasts and rarely what one expects it to be. Take the climate. When one arrives in Istanbul, instead of being met by that sticky heat so typical of the Orient, and so conducive to idling, one may encounter snow flurries in March, a pea-souper that has all the foghorns blaring in October, or a howling southerly wind in December. But that does not stop the almond trees from blossoming in January, nor Indian summer from shining through the storms until the end of November. One can go swimming in the Mediterranean at Antalya until the end of autumn, when the temperature is already -30°C (-23°F) at Erzurum in the north-east.

History has left many traces in Turkey: columns from cities that were first Greek and later Roman tower above the land from west to east. Most were rebuilt in later centuries as part of the grandiose designs of philhellenic kings from the now-forgotten Commagene, Adiabene and Osroene kingdoms - such as the colossal heads of Nemrut Dağ. Minarets soar delicately into the sky throughout the country. Images appear everywhere of Byzantium's stern-looking saints - the warrior saints with curly black beards and the Anchorites with long white beards - who appear to be engaged in a confrontation between Christendom and Islam. In Turkey's past, one finds a maze of early civilizations - Lydian, Phrygian, Carian, Lycian, Assyrian, Urartian. Even further back, one discovers evidence of the Hittites, and then of constructions from among the oldest known human settlements, dating from around 6500 BC.

Turkey's people in all their rich variety have managed a rare achievement, a true synthesis of past and present, of East and West, almost despite themselves. They are farmers who have been cast into the maelstrom of the modern world through their ten million television sets and dozen channels; through the village telephone booth a coin's call away from Strasbourg, Hamburg or Jeddah; or the fax at the post office that receives money orders from children now emigrated abroad. They are city-dwellers rushing headlong into a mechanical, electronic era. They are Moslems convinced that Captain Jacques Cousteau embraced Islam after finding the truth written in the Koran at the bottom of the sea, and they happily start up theological discussions with foreigners under palm trees at street cafés. They are women who veil themselves out of pride and unveil themselves out of curiosity, who work in fields, in offices and in factories. In short, Turkey is a world of people and things that constantly provokes a host of questions for the visitor and challenges one's preconceptions at every moment.

The Ortaköy Mosque built in 1855 by the Armenian architect Nigoghos Balyan is dwarfed by the first bridge to span the Bosphorus (completed in 1973).

People may claim that Istanbul is not all there is to Turkey, just as New York is not the only city to visit in the United States nor Rome the sole place to see in Italy. But Istanbul is the country's heart. As cities go, Istanbul ranks with Rome as one of the most universal and legendary. Moreover, it is a true *polis*, the epitome of a city. The name Istanbul actually means "to the city" (*eis tin polin*). The fact that it was crowned the New Rome - a title which its Orthodox Patriarch still uses - is appropriate, for the place where Istanbul stands was and is, above all, a place fit for the ruling of an empire, as well as a unique natural site.

Istanbul's location, dominating the Bosphorus, has always allowed its rulers to control maritime routes leading from the Black Sea, where many ancient land routes converged - the Silk Road coming from the east and running along the northern shore of the Caspian Sea, the Fur Road coming from the north across the steppes, and the Amber Road that came down from the Baltic to the mouth of the Danube. Newer routes also pass through here, such as the Baku-Batum oil pipeline and other pipelines that will bring oil and natural gas from Central Asia to the Mediterranean and Europe in the near future. Istanbul is also a passageway between Asia and Europe, one the first hominids used on their journey to Europe when the northern part of the Black Sea was still frozen. Xerxes crossed the Bosphorus on a legendary floating bridge on his way to conquer Greece. Today, people cross it on two suspension bridges.

Istanbul's site is an arid promontory that juts out into and blocks off the extreme southern end of the Bosphorus, intercepting the paths of passing boats and ferries. It was here that Greek colonists settled in the 7th century BC. They had come from Megara, now a dusty town in Athens' industrial suburbs. Byzantium, the Megaran colony, resisted the Athenian fleet, Philip of Macedon's army, Alexander's Diadochi and the Romans, until it was finally taken and destroyed in 196 by the Emperor Septimius Severus, who hastily rebuilt it. Chosen by Constantine as capital of the Eastern Roman Empire and renamed Constantinople in 330, it remained for sixteen centuries, until 1924, the capital of an empire that stretched from Hungary to the Caucasus, from the Crimea to Arabia, from Mesopotamia to North Africa - an empire constantly expanding or shrinking with its changing fortunes.

Under Justinian and his immediate successors, Constantinople's influence extended all the way to Italy and Spain. But it was eventually forced to give up the other bank of the Golden Horn to the Genoese, and the Bosphorus to the Turks a few years before the Ottoman conquest. During the reign of the great sultans in the 16th century, Constantinople's domain extended from the gates of Vienna to Yemen, but ultimately it was unable to control its own home

The silkworm cocoon caravanserai at Bursa. In the foreground, the dome of the hamam built by Sultan Orhan (1326-62). PRECEDING PAGES: The far end of the peninsula is the site of Istanbul proper. In the foreground on the right, the mosque built by Sultan Ahmet (1604-1617), called the Blue Mosque. In the centre, Haghia Sophia and behind it the Topkapı Palace with its tower overlooking the Council Hall. In the foreground on the left is the site of the Byzantine Hippodrome where the obelisk now stands. In the background, the entrance to the Bosphorus and its first suspension bridge. On the left, the entrance to the Golden Horn and on the right, the approach to the Sea of Marmara.

The Blue Mosque and Haghia Sophia aligned; although 1,080 years separate their construction, the two buildings display their architectural affinities. Between them, on the right, the hamam of Roxelana, Süleyman the Magnificent's wife, built by the architect Sinan in 1556.

"**H**alt, wayfarer; the land over which your feet have been treading so lightly has seen the fall of an era," says the inscription written on the mountain at the site of the battle of the Dardanelles. Messages like this one, painstakingly written in stone by soldiers, can be found throughout Turkey.

territory as the last of the Ottomans fought against Turkish nationalists based in Ankara - and lost. When Ankara became the official capital of the Turkish Republic in 1923, Constantinople was looked upon with suspicion and condescension. It was officially renamed Istanbul in 1930. The city had been the largest in Europe in the 11th century during the Comnenus dynasty and again from the 16th to the 18th century, when London caught up with it, followed by Paris a century later. In the 17th century it most probably had a population of 700,000, while it had no more than 850,000 inhabitants at the beginning of the 20th century. Istanbul only reached the million mark between 1945 and 1950. Today, it has more than seven million inhabitants.

The new Turkey of 1923, weak and drained after twelve years of war, desperately needed a new generation to help it achieve its potential. World War II, with its restrictions and hardships, prolonged the stagnation in Turkey. After the war, however, dramatic demographic changes began to alter Istanbul's form and character, and the mechanization of farming practices, which drove many tenant farmers off the land, did the rest. The first shanty towns sprouted around Istanbul in 1947. Fifteen years later, more than 40 per cent of the population were living in them. At the end of the 1940s there were still vegetable gardens inside Istanbul's 5th-century walls. Outside the walls there was only a ring of cemeteries.

Today, greater Istanbul is a *terra incognita* even for those who think they know the city. Venturing into new neighbourhoods in the periphery that have not yet appeared on maps is always an adventure. An isolated monument in the countryside - a stone bridge or an aqueduct - may suddenly find itself surrounded by modern buildings as the urban front advances inexorably into the fields and meadows, followed by roads, power lines and bus routes, but rarely by proper water pipelines.

Now the city and its suburbs stretch along more than 150 km. (93 miles) of shoreline, from Silivri on the European side of the Sea of Marmara to Gebze on the Asian side. And though Ankara is still Turkey's political capital, Istanbul remains the centre of the country's industrial and financial power, of its artistic and cultural activity, of its press, publishing and tourism.

The reopening of the Black Sea to international trade has enhanced Istanbul's strategic position but created new risks: the Bosphorus, 32 km. (20 miles) long, is only about 700 metres (2,300 ft.) wide at the point where the first Ottoman sultans built their castles in order to control the sea route, and its banks are almost entirely built up. But this Grand Canal is used not just by local vessels, fishing boats, yachts, outboard motor boats and other small boats of all kinds, but by large ferries and even oil tankers and container ships, whose numbers are ever increasing. Accidents involving ships ramming the wooden houses built on the banks are common, as are fires from oil tankers, putting the city constantly in peril from a new, 20th-century menace.

Istanbul is a historic city now engulfed by contemporary Third World urban sprawl: gigantic traffic jams, hilltops covered with houses that have sprouted up seemingly overnight and stretch as far as the eye can see, along with office buildings and hotel towers, and odd gaps in the city centre meant to be a show of modernism. But despite such "progress", innumerable craftsmen can still be found working in back courtyards and on the upper floors of old buildings, evidence of the vitality of the city's traditions. This fascinating mixture of ancient and modern is a major source of the city's charm.

Another is Istanbul's dramatic setting: the city's silhouette is one of domes and minarets hovering above the green waters of the Bosphorus, basically unchanged for centuries (if one ignores the high-rise blocks and housing estates in the background). The city's long history can be seen everywhere - if one looks beneath the surface. The old Constantinople of turn-of-the-century French writer Pierre Loti, with its quiet alleyways where furtive movements were glimpsed behind windows covered with wire mesh, is gone forever. Loti himself was already bemoaning the loss at the time he was writing. But, while strolling down a noisy street full of beggars and incessant traffic, one may still come upon the quiet courtyard of a mosque, a Byzantine church or simply a small café with a vine arbour, and suddenly the city lifts its modern veil to reveal its ancient face.

Istanbul has steadily grown since the 1950s and has been patiently rebuilding its infrastructure to cope with its new population. By the year 2000 it could once again be the largest city in Europe. The autoroute under construction that will link Istanbul with Edirne on the northern border and with Ankara in the heart of Anatolia has made it an inevitable stop along the route for all land traffic from Europe to Asia. Maritime traffic from Bulgaria and Romania, as well as from Moldavia, the Ukraine, the Caucasus and even Russia, is obliged to pass through the Bosphorus on its way to and from the Black Sea. In fact, Istanbul is already the gateway to the West for these countries, whose citizens can be seen every day in the city's marketplaces and squares, buying and selling all kinds of objects. This dynamism and change has naturally spilled over beyond the city to the banks of the Sea of Marmara, between the Bosphorus and the Dardanelles, and into neighbouring cities. The Sea of Marmara, with its islands and natural beauty, has already become a holiday destination for people from Istanbul.

Two other former capitals of the Ottoman Empire, Bursa and Edirne, would, like Istanbul, barely be recognized by their past residents. Bursa, whose name means "the green", built on the slopes of Turkey's Mount Olympus (Uludağ), was indeed a city filled with greenery until the end of the 1960s. Its alleyways were lined with wooden houses, mosque complexes and other religious buildings built by the first sultans, and with open spaces and gardens. Many

Rumelifeneri Fortress at the northern entrance to the Bosphorus. This fortification, which French engineers helped to construct, was built in the 18th century to ward off a possible attack by the Russians. Until recently its location was part of a restricted military zone.

Seraskerat Arch,
formerly the grand
entrance to the
Ottoman Ministry of
Defence, a complex
now occupied by
Istanbul University.
In the foreground, the
20th-century Beyazıt
square, where student
demonstrations were
held during the 1960s.
Today it is the site
of a flea market with
vendors from the ex-
Soviet Union. Citizens
of Russia, the Ukraine,
the Caucasus and
Central Asia come
here to sell their
bric-a-brac and return
home loaded down
with products from the
capitalist world.

of these monuments are still standing today, and, as in most of Turkey, have been carefully preserved. Unfortunately, they are surrounded by noisy traffic and hastily constructed modern buildings, along with a few rare examples of older houses. The great Ottoman funerary complexes, however, whose greenery has been protected by enclosing walls, have remained intact. So has the city's bazaar, where the expansion of new buildings was halted by the caravanserai's bulk, and where the extraordinary variety of wares found in the market, along with its sheer density of population, have enabled it to achieve a balance, albeit precarious, between old and new.

Edirne, whose position as a frontier town prevented rapid urban growth, has retained more of its past character. Located at the meeting point of three countries - Bulgaria, Greece and Turkey - and of three rivers - the Maritza, the Arda and the Tundza - Edirne was the heart of historic Thrace. Full of monuments from the early Ottoman period, its attractions include an architectural gem, the Selimiye Mosque, the architect Sinan's masterpiece. The city has largely retained the air of a provincial Ottoman city, with its cosy neighbourhoods and lively bazaar; the ruins of Beyazıt II's old palace and its adjacent complex have also survived.

A 250-km. (150-mile) imperial highway once connected Istanbul and Edirne. Each stop along the way was marked by grandiose monuments, many of which remain, such as the Lüleburgaz complex, which includes a mosque, court school and marketplace built in the mid-16th century by Sinan for the Grand Vizier Sokollu Mehmet Paşa. Another example is the three-arch ("humpback") bridge built by the same architect at Büyük Çekmece on the edge of urban Istanbul. Travel between Istanbul and Mudanya, Bursa's port, was traditionally by sea, as the trip over land was lengthened by the need to follow the coastline of the Gulf of Nicomedia.

Although the Thracian countryside between Istanbul and Edirne is somewhat harsh - with a succession of gently rolling hills barely brightened by fields of sunflowers - the countryside near Bursa and the surrounding area is greatly varied. It includes Mount Olympus and its foothills, where there are many colourful villages to discover - such as Cumalıkızık - as well as many beautiful lakes. Lake Iznik, for instance, is worth going out of one's way to visit, both for its natural beauty and for the lakeside city of Iznik, formerly Nicaea. The city, preserved within its still-intact Roman walls, contains an ancient theatre, Byzantine churches and proto-Ottoman mosques. One can sit by the lake at sunset to enjoy a dinner of grilled fish and a bottle of wine, and easily imagine why the Church Fathers found this the ideal place in which to gather for the great ecumenical council held in 325.

The throne room at Dolmabahçe Palace on the Bosphorus, to which the Ottoman imperial court was transferred from the the Topkapı Palace in 1855.

The Topkapı Palace consists of a maze of buildings constructed over a period of centuries. The buildings surrounding the large cypress-filled courtyard (centre background) date from the 15th century; the courtyard with arcades as well as the little buildings surrounding it date from the 18th century; and the neoclassical tower of the Council Hall, or divan, dates from the early 19th century. The harem lies within the main body of buildings in the foreground below the wall on the right; the tops of these buildings can be seen between the Council Tower and the high dome, which has a frail minaret next to it. The harem overlooks a room that contains relics of the Prophet Mohammed. Behind the tower is the far end of the palace's second courtyard, used for ceremonies, with the throne room (the four-sided sloping roof to the left of the tower) at the back of the courtyard. Further back is a third, private courtyard with the library and treasury opening onto it.

The Topkapı Palace. The three arches seen in the foreground provide access to the passageway connecting the third courtyard to the harem, of which only the roofs of the service buildings are visible here. The building with a dormer window is the black eunuchs' dormitory. The one to its right is the princes' school. The first open area behind that is the courtyard of the women of the harem; the second one below it is the hospital courtyard. On the right, a corner of the Queen Mother's courtyard, through which the upper section of the harem can be reached. In the foreground, giving onto the palace's second courtyard, can be seen the eight domes of the outer treasury where Janissaries gathered every three months to be paid. On the extreme left, the domes of the Council Hall.

The Topkapı
Palace's third
courtyard. In the
foreground, the library
built by Ahmet III
in 1718. In the centre
background, four
domes cover what
must have been the
winter quarters for the
original core of the
palace, begun in 1468
by Mehmet II, the
conqueror of the city.
The room with the
elevated dome, which
may originally have
been the imperial
chambers, today
contains relics of the
Prophet Mohammed.
Behind it rise the
Baghdad Pavilion at
the far end and the
Revan Pavilion to the
right around the
marble courtyard,
commemorating the
capture of the cities of
Erivan and Baghdad
by Murad IV in 1635
and 1638 respectively.

Haghia Sophia, built by the Emperor Justinian between the spring of 532 and December 537, is unique in Byzantine architecture. The building was restored many times under Byzantine and Ottoman rulers, altering its appearance. The three domed buildings on the left are the mausoleums of Selim II (1566-74), Murad III (1574-95), and Mehmet III (1595- 1603). Mehmet II, the Conqueror, who converted the church to a mosque, had the brick minaret built. The second minaret, in the foreground, was added by Beyazıt II (1481-1512) and the other two by Selim II. Above, Haghia Sophia's central dome and apse, altered by the addition of buttresses. None of Istanbul's other mosques has a dome to rival this one, which is 31 metres (101 ft.) in diameter and reaches a height of 56 metres (183 ft.).

Multiple minarets, were the privilege of royal and imperial mosques. The courtyard of the Blue Mosque, equal in area to that of the prayer-hall, was also used as a place for prayers for large congregations; ceremonies were also held here during imperial visits for Friday prayers. Imperial mosques had monumental entrances for ceremonial occasions, that led directly to the main courtyard and from there into the prayer-hall, as well as side entrances with direct access to the prayer-hall. The cistern in the middle of the Blue Mosque's courtyard, which was not intended for performing ritual ablutions, is on a much reduced scale.

Ever since the conquest of Constantinople, Ottoman architecture has derived its inspiration from the structure of Haghia Sophia: a main central dome with two half-domes on the side of the narthex and the apse. This design was suitable for the rectangular plan of a basilica but not for the basic form of a mosque, where worshippers range themselves in parallel rows facing the wall incorporating the mihrab (prayer niche) and indicating the direction of Mecca. Ottoman architects then changed the roof design in order to create a rectangular ground-plan, or at least a square one. The square plan gave rise to the kind of symmetrical roof with a central dome and four half-domes characteristic of the Blue Mosque, the plan of which forms two squares – one the building itself and the other the courtyard.

Ottoman religious architecture is characterized by vast and uninterrupted interiors covered with an interplay of domes in a myriad of styles. While in Byzantine architecture the roof is visibly supported by pillars and columns that maintain arches, vaults and domes, in Ottoman architecture the weight of the roof is progressively shifted to the sides of the construction in order to open up the inner space as much as possible. In a Byzantine building, the structural elements create a play of shadows and light, which encourages meditation and individual prayer. In an Ottoman building, in contrast, the interior is luminous and open, designed for communal prayer. The exterior of an Ottoman building typically includes a pyramid-shaped system of domes and half-domes flowing downward and outward from the central dome, as seen here in the Blue Mosque.

Çirağan Palace, built in 1870 for Sultan Abdülaziz, was destroyed by fire during the night of January 6, 1910. Its gutted shell loomed over the banks of the Bosphorus for seventy years until a Japanese company decided to transform it into a five-star hotel. Although the building itself has been rather well restored, the design of the surrounding area probably has little in common with its original appearance.

The Grand Bazaar reveals its labyrinthine form when seen from the air. This market complex dates back to the years following the Ottoman conquest, and by the end of the 15th century it already contained close to 2,000 shops. The complex has been destroyed several times by fire and earthquakes and then rebuilt, adding to its apparently disorderly layout. Generally speaking, however, the upper areas are alleyways and the lower ones are shops.

The Grand Bazaar with Nuruosmaniye Mosque (completed in 1754) in the foreground. The domes of the two bedesten, substantial stone buildings used for the sale of valuable objects, both dating from 1460-70, stand out among the other roofs. The bedesten in the background is used today by jewellers and antique dealers, while auctions are held in the one in the foreground.

The Süleymaniye
Mosque was built
between 1550 and
1557 for Süleyman
the Magnificent. It is
composed of a socio-
religious complex
of four medrese
(colleges), a Koranic
school, a medical
school, an insane
asylum, a soup
kitchen, and a hamam
(steam bath), as well
as the mausoleums of
the sovereign and his
wife Herrem Sultan
(Roxelana), located
behind the mosque.
The mosque's design
was based on that of
Haghia Sophia,
including a central
dome and two half-
domes supporting it,
with a monumental
courtyard in front.

The Beyazıt II mosque complex with the Grand Bazaar in the background. The mosque, completed in 1505, resembles those in Bursa and Edirne in several ways, particularly in its adjacent dependencies, where the dervishes lived. To the left of the mosque is the former soup kitchen, now the National Library. Between the two lies the second-hand booksellers' market.

The Aqueduct of Valens (364-378), the oldest standing monument in the city, brought water from nearby springs to the Roman city located at the far end of the peninsula. Redesigned by the Ottomans, who strengthened the water conveyance system with an impressive network of canals and aqueducts, it continued to carry water until modern times.

Galata Tower is part of the fortifications built by the Genoese in 1349 in the upper part of the Latin city facing Constantinople across the Golden Horn. Surrendered to the Ottoman Turks in 1453, it was first used as a jail for Christian slaves, then as a fire station, and currently it houses a nightclub with a breathtaking view of the city. The country's first Western-style building was erected in the 19th century in Galata, which at the time of the Genoese already contained several large houses. Extensive modernization followed shortly thereafter.

Beneath the minaret rising from the modern building in the foreground is the oldest building in Galata. The basement of the former Byzantine castle, where the end of a mountain range closed off the Golden Horn, was converted to a mosque. In the 17th century, the larger mosque behind it replaced the church of St. Claire, which had supplanted a Greek church, Aghia Photini. The latter church had been built on the site of a temple of Artemis Photodhotis, giver of light. Over 2,000 years of history are encapsulated in this ordinary neighbourhood with its modern grey asphalt and yellow shared taxis.

This park was laid out to replace the neighbourhood between Haghia Sophia and the Blue Mosque, destroyed by fire at the beginning of the century. On the left, the hamam built by Sinan is now used as a carpet showroom. In the background, the Blue Mosque's medrese and to its right the mausoleum of its founder, Ahmet I. Further to the right is the copper-covered dome of the fountain presented by Kaiser Wilhelm II to Sultan Abdül Hamit II on his visit to Istanbul in 1895.

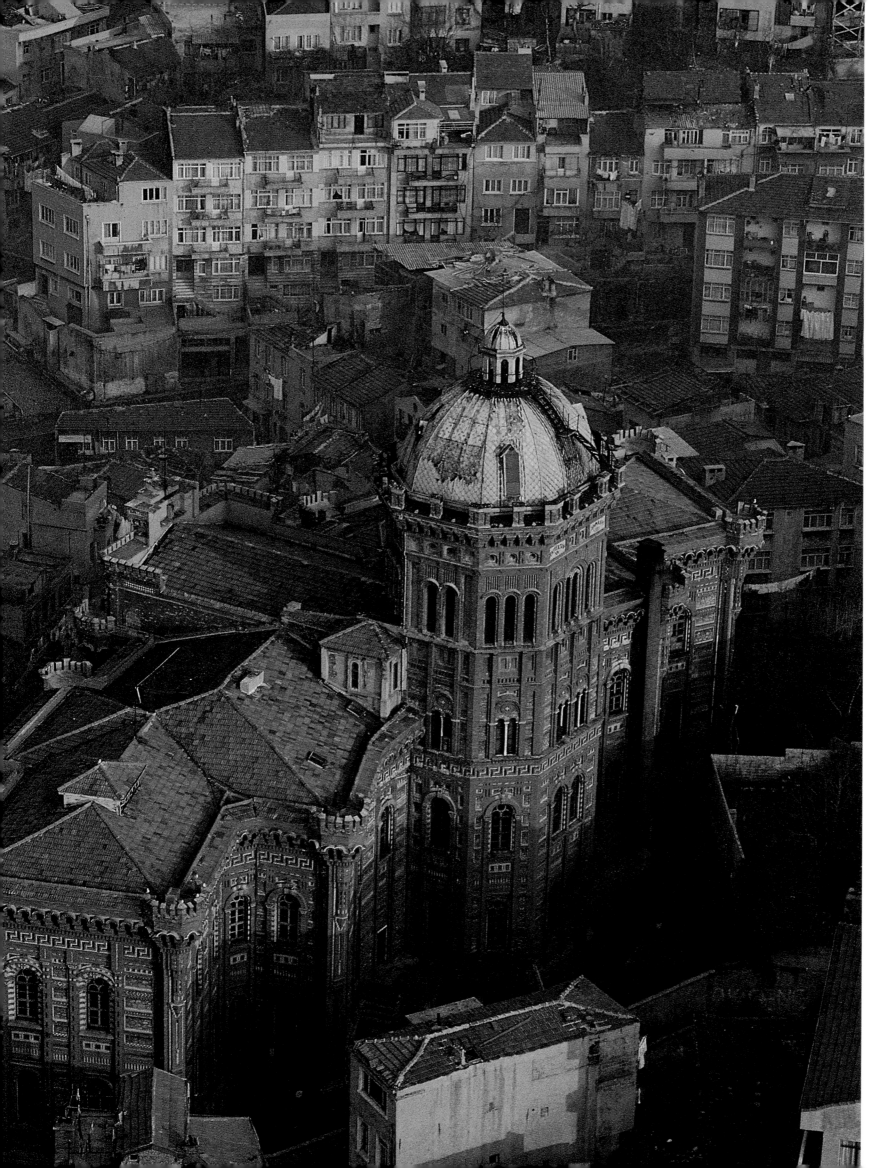

The Greek secondary school, built in the mid-19th century in the upper Phanar quarter near the Orthodox patriarchate. The homes of members of the Greek aristocracy, called Phanariots, provided the Ottoman administration with skilled interpreters and even royalty, such as the princes of Wallachia and Moldavia. The buildings dating from the 1960s now mainly accommodate recent immigrants from Anatolia.

FOLLOWING PAGES : The three parts of modern Istanbul. In the foreground, the old city with Topkapı Palace on the right; beyond the Golden Horn (left) is Galata, and across the Bosphorus on the Asian shore is Üsküdar.

The Fortress of the Seven Towers (Yedikule). Originally part of the Byzantine fortifications, it was enlarged after the Ottoman conquest by Mehmet II. First used as the imperial treasury, it was transformed into a prison for high-level captives, including ambassadors from countries at war with the Ottoman Empire, Knights of St. John of Malta and other illustrious prisoners for whom huge ransoms were demanded, Ottoman dignitaries, and even a sultan, Osman II, who was strangled to death here in 1622.

From the middle of the 18th century Ottoman architecture was influenced greatly by western styles, which affected the buildings' external appearance more than their basic layout. There are both a baroque and a neo-classical Ottoman style; in the latter, the Balyan family of architects excelled, and over four generations of them built the majority of the imperial palaces along the Bosphorus, including the main palace of Dolmabahçe that replaced Topkapı in 1855. Here, despite the neo-classical pediments, Versailles-style balustrade and neo-Renaissance windows, the public buildings on the left are clearly separated, in the traditional manner, by the huge throne room and by a wall from the harem on the right.

Different kinds of buildings at Arnavutköy on the western shore of the Bosphorus. In the foreground, traditional wooden houses dating from the beginning of the century are flanked by more recent constructions. In the middle of the modern buildings behind them is a Greek church. Behind that, a traditional-style house and another building under construction that will most likely be finished with a traditional façade (TOP). BOTTOM: On the left, a country house from the 1950s. On the right, a neo-traditional house whose right wing has preserved the spirit of a yalı, the typical house on the waterfront of the Bosphorus, allowing visitors direct access from the water when they arrived in caiques.

At the turn of the century, the architecture of wooden Ottoman houses was influenced by colonial and Indo-Moghul styles that came via Brighton and Deauville, as evidenced in buildings designed by European or Levantine architects. This complex, built to house a European embassy, is used today as the President of the Republic's official summer residence (TOP). BOTTOM: The second building on the left is a classic Ottoman residence. The one on the far right is a particularly exuberant specimen of Oriental-influenced style designed by Alexandre Vallaury (1850-1921), an architect of French extraction who was born and lived his whole life in Constantinople except for the period of his university studies in Paris. He played a considerable part in reviving Ottoman architecture (he also designed the little mosque behind the house).

The landing stage on the largest of the Princes' Islands (Büyükada), flanked by small hotels, cafés and restaurants. The island in the Sea of Marmara was the favourite resort of the Levantine aristocracy in the 19th century and continues to be a highly sought-after spot in summer.

The little port of Sarıyer on the European shore of the upper Bosphorus owes its attraction to its fish market (under the corrugated iron roofs on the left), where supplies of the freshest fish in the environs of Istanbul are to be found, and to the many cafés and restaurants near the waterfront. People from the city come here for Sunday outings.

The famous Green Mausoleum of Bursa, which has turned blue since being restored. In the interest of creating a pedestrian area between the mausoleum and the mosque to the left, both built under Mehmet I (1413-21), a tunnel had to be dug on the right. However, the little block of houses with a hamam in their midst retains its charm.

The mosque of Emir Sultan, a place of pilgrimage which takes its name from a holy figure buried here, the son-in-law and counsellor of Sultan Beyazıt I, known as "the Thunderbolt" (1389-1402). The original mosque was destroyed by an earthquake. The present one, which replaced it in 1804, was built in an archaic style; the courtyard's wooden portico with its pointed arches is in the Ottoman "baroque" style.

Bursa, a "green" city, had been little changed by time until two decades ago, but today it is an industrial metropolis with about a million inhabitants. The few historic remains are its monuments dating from the beginning of the Ottoman era and its old centre, which has undergone restoration. The mosque on the right, built by Sultan Orhan (1326-60), is the oldest known Ottoman royal mosque. In the middle are two large caravanserais: the one for silkworm cocoons (Koza Han) built in 1490 provides a reminder of the city's former chief activity; and the one behind it for plants (Fidan Han), dating back to 1460. Inside each courtyard there is a small oratory, one polygonal, one cylindrical. In the left foreground, the hamam of Orhan.
FOLLOWING PAGES: A snow-covered Mount Olympus landscape behind Bursa.

The modern town of Çanakkale on the Asian shore of the Dardanelles took its name from this fortress, built under Mehmet II (1451-81) to block the passage of ships, a task which it effectively fulfilled until the battle of the Dardanelles in 1915. The little village that grew up around the fortress has since developed into a large town that is now the county seat.

Mehmet II built the fortress of Kilid'ül-Bahr (Sea Lock) on the European shore opposite Çanakkale to close off the entrance to the Dardanelles. Its trefoil plan, with a triangular central tower, is unique in Ottoman architecture, since fortresses were quite rare. The outer walls and the tower in the foreground were built under Süleyman the Magnificent (1520-66).

THE COAST AND ANTIQUITY

Turkey's Aegean coastline is one of the most historic frontiers in the world. Like all border regions, it is made up of complementary and contrasting elements, of relationships that are tranquil and symbiotic as well as ones that are violently antagonistic. The roots of these relationships reach far back into history and even into the prehistoric era. The Aegean as we know it is really only a collapsed plain - an extension of the valleys of Asia Minor and of Greece's massifs; its islands are former mountain peaks. Thus, the large islands near the coast represent the natural extension of the peninsulas that jut out into the sea. The sea, for its part, penetrates the mainland through long jagged bays resulting from the flooding of valleys. Both sailors in the coastal waters and shepherds on land naturally had to follow the contours of these land masses, giving rise to the ancient civilizations whose traces still dot the landscape. Conflicts originating here have reached far beyond the region. Ever since the time of Homer, the confrontation of East with West has been focused in this area.

The Trojan War marked the beginning of the era during which Greek colonists, both from the continent and the islands, settled on the coast of Asia Minor. The opulence of the civilization they created, which was sustained by the sea and the fertile land, is still visible in the vestiges of its monuments, and its sophistication can be measured by the importance of the philosophers, poets and historians who were born here. But an Aegean civilization established on both sides of the sea could only antagonize those living on the vast tracts of the interior. The first such confrontation was with the Persians. Greece held fast and even took its revenge for Persian attacks on Greek settlements through the victorious campaigns of Alexander the Great of Macedon. Hellenistic civilization spread all the way to the Indus River, while absorbing Oriental influences. Hellenization was often superficial, however, and, despite the Grecian place names in this area that were recorded by Greek and Roman geographers, the traces of Greek temples and columns are limited to the coast and the valleys along the Aegean and Mediterranean shores of Asia Minor. What better way to measure how far Greece's influence really extended?

The Pax Romana promoted prosperity in Asia Minor, where an urban network that had already been established reached the high point in its development. The Roman Empire relied on this Oriental network greatly during the period of its gradual decline and its increasing domination by the West. It is understandable that Constantine chose to move his capital east, to Constantinople. The Roman Empire eventually adopted Christianity and was altered by oriental influences, but it continued to defend its Greco-Roman heritage. The Byzantine Empire would last for another thousand years, but the urban network of western Asia Minor fell apart much

Rock tombs overlooking the sea at Kalkan on the Lycian coast between Patara and Kaş. A typical Mediterranean landscape combining scrub, rocks, and an emerald green sea, with a few ancient remains to make the perfect holiday picture.

faster, the region proving incapable of maintaining its possessions or of withstanding Arab and Turkish assaults. When Turkic tribes moved down into the valleys that led to the Aegean and established settlements, this area once again became a border region. This time it was Latin peoples - Venetians, Genoese, the Knights of St. John of Rhodes - who ruled the islands, instead of exhausted Byzantium. The alliance of the Anatolian Turkic emirates under the Ottomans once again broke up the border, but this time in the other direction. Greece and the islands now belonged to the Ottomans, who pushed on beyond the Balkans. The Anatolian people, having already experienced Hellenic, Roman and Christian influences, were converted to Islam. Mixing with the newcomers, they were assimilated into the new culture and influenced it n turn, in a symbiotic process whose results can still be seen today.

The new unification of the Aegean region failed to halt migrations of settlers, mainly from Greece into Asia Minor. During the 18th century and at the beginning of the 19th, before Greece existed as a nation and even afterwards, Greeks once again colonized Turkey's coastal cities and even established settlements inland along the valleys. There, they mixed with the local Moslem population and with Christians from inland Anatolia, in particular from Cappadocia. A flourishing Aegean economy began to develop through trade in crops such as grapes, figs and cotton, aided by the railways that were built beginning in the mid-19th century to connect the interior with the coast.

These immigrants remained a minority - except in a few specific places on the coast - but their economic power increased to the point of becoming dominant by the turn of the 20th century. After Greece annexed the large islands off Turkey's coast in 1912, the Aegean border issue cropped up once again and brought about a new conflict that lasted from 1919 to 1922. The enforced return to Greece of Greeks living in Turkey, and of Turks living in Greece to Turkey, brought the curtain down again between the islands and the continent. The Aegean border between Greece and Turkey reverted to what it had been three thousand years earlier, leaving an accumulation of indelible traces from both cultures on both sides of the official dividing line.

Whereas Turkey's western coastal region is composed of alternating mountain ranges perpendicular to the coast, prolonged by peninsulas and valleys ending in deep bays, its Mediterranean coastline runs parallel to one range, the Taurus Mountains. The interweaving mountain ranges form a knot that ends in the abrupt shores on the Lycian and Pamphylian coasts between Fethiye and Antalya at the south-western corner of Anatolia.

The relative importance of the cities located where the valleys open out to the sea was determined by the valleys' orientation, depth and communication links with the Anatolian plateau. These

Izmir, formerly Smyrna, a cosmopolitan city with a Frankish, Greek, Armenian and Turkish population, was the Ottoman Empire's leading port for exports until 1920, when a Greek administration was installed after World War I.

factors gradually made Izmir, formerly Smyrna, the most important city in the region. It has been the last stop on the caravan route from Persia since the 17th century, and in the 19th century a railway network was built to transport produce from inland. At the end of the Ottoman Empire, it was the country's foremost port for exports. With its industrial and trade activities and its population of two million, Izmir today is ranked as the third most important city in the country after Istanbul and Ankara.

Kuşadası, formerly Scalanuova, a small port that replaced Ephesus after the latter was cut off from the sea. It has recently become a thriving tourist centre, site of the first Club Méditerrané in Turkey. The fortress was built in the 14th century by the Menteşe Turkic emirate.

Rapid urbanization has so far failed to completely destroy Izmir's traditional Aegean lifestyle. Its ancient districts remain as well: the Frankish and Greek quarters (burned down in 1922 and subsequently rebuilt) and the Turkish quarter that still clings to the side of the hill where the ancient city was located at the foot of the citadel.

On the northern Aegean coast lies the peninsula on which the ancient sites of Scamander and Troy were established. Today this area is very rural and inhabited by Turkic peoples who have retained elements of their former nomadic lifestyle as well as their syncretic myths, such as that of the blond nymph (Sarıkız) of Kaz daği, or Mount Ida. On the southern side, Assos is one of the region's most important landmarks from the past.

On a bay facing the Greek island of Lesbos is Edremit, known for its olive groves. At the southern entrance of the bay, the city of Ayvalık and its small archipelago - entirely Greek before 1922 - have retained a unique, well-preserved style of domestic architecture. To the south lies the Bay of Çandarlı where the valley of Pergamum opens out to the sea. Now called Bergama, a sub-prefecture of Izmir, Pergamum was the capital of the Hellenistic kingdom of the same name and a mecca of Aegean civilization. The people of the Turkic up-country, like inhabitants of all inland areas in the Aegean region, produce beautiful rugs and *kilims,* which once greatly contributed to the prosperity of Izmir, their export centre during the 19th century.

Foça, at the entrance of the Bay of Izmir, is the ancient city of Phocaea; a Genoese colony at the end of the Middle Ages, Phocaea was a centre for alum exports. Izmir is located at the opening of the Gediz valley, which is the deepest indentation along this coast and leads to the Anatolian plateau. Sardis, capital of the Lydian kingdom of Croesus, can be found on a highway that follows the valley upward. Further north, on the Istanbul road, lies Manisa, capital of a Turkic emirate in the 14th century, where Murat III (1574-95) built an imperial mosque.

The Çeşme peninsula, along the southern end of the Bay of Izmir, is the most imposing peninsula on the Aegean coast. Formed of a multitude of promontories and creeks, it has a number of small towns and fishing villages. The Bay of Kuşadası lies to the south, between the Çeşme peninsula and the Greek island of Samos. It forms the mouth of Küçük

Kayaköy, formerly
Lyvissi, a town whose
Greek inhabitants
were deported during
World War I. Unlike
other places similarly
affected, such as
Makri (now Fethiye),
Kayaköy was
abandoned and not
repopulated by Turks
coming from Greece.
Recently, Istanbul
residents have begun
buying abandoned
houses here and
turning them into
summer homes.

The fortress of Marmaris, founded in 1522, surrounded by a modern town. A small amphitheatre can be seen at the centre of the complex.

Menderes, the ancient site of Caystros, with Ephesus, landlocked by centuries of silting, further inland. A small promontory of which the island of Samos - located about 1 mile off the coast - is an extension, separates the mouth of the Caystre from that of the Maeander, and was the site of the ancient cities of Miletus and Priene. The ruins of these cities, which once were located on the coast, are also inland today. The varied Aegean coastline continues to the south with the Bodrum and Marmaris peninsulas.

This area is the Carian coast, particularly rugged and picturesque, where a combination of natural beauty and ancient sites has led to a rapid development of tourism facilities in recent years.

The less jagged Lycian and Pamphylian coasts with their mountainous interiors have been opened up more recently to tourism. Here, residents of both ancient cities and modern villages have been completely centred on the sea, whereas inhabitants of the sparsely populated interior have always been and still are involved solely in farming. One must go all the way east along the coast to Antalya, to the end of the bay of the same name, to reach the plains and an opening towards the Anatolian plateau. There, prestigious ancient sites can be found in abundance - Perge, Aspendos and Side. Antalya and Alanya, the latter the westernmost site on this part of the Turkish coast, are essentially Seljuk cities. Just beyond Alanya lies the natural barrier of the Taurus range, known in ancient times as Rough Cilicia; a modern highway now runs between the mountains and the sea. In the Taurus, three kingdoms once joined at a point on the road leading from the Seljuk capital of Konya to the Mediterranean: the Turkic Karaman emirate, which had taken refuge from its hereditary Ottoman enemy at Mut and Silifke; the Armenian kingdom of Cilicia, which reached all the way to the maritime castle of Corycos; and the Cypriot kingdom of the Lusignans, who had established a fortress at the southernmost tip of Asia Minor, at Anamur.

The plains reach towards the coast again at Mersin, which is also Turkey's leading port along this stretch of coastline. At Mersin begins the plain of Çukurova, covered with cotton plantations and source for the textile industry centred around Adana, Turkey's fourth-largest city. Upper Mesopotamia, Syria and the Bay of Alexandrette lie just to the east, but seemingly another world away. Beyond Amanus is the low valley of Oronte, annexed by Turkey in 1939, whose major city is Antakya (formerly Antioch), a city with a particularly rich past.

Turkey's coastal regions are, along with the Istanbul area, the most developed part of the country. Largely mechanized farming combined with industry and tourism have attracted migrant workers from all over the country. Despite the rapid growth, however, many rural customs and ways of life have endured.

The historic site of Troy, where nine successive, superimposed cities were hastily excavated from 1870 on by Heinrich Schliemann, a German industrialist. It has few remaining monuments to excite the imagination of those hoping to relive Homer's epic. But the Trojan Horse has been brought back to life - for the benefit of tourists.

Pergamum
(now Bergama) was
the capital of the most
brilliant of all the
Hellenistic kingdoms
in Asia from 281
to 133 BC, and one
of the largest Anatolian
cities. In the plains
about 1 kilometre
(1100 yds) from the
city lies the
Aesclepion, a vast
healing complex
made up chiefly
of a central courtyard
with porticos,
and, in opposite
corners, a theatre
and the Temple of
Aesclepius (god of
medecine).

In the foreground, the Temple of Aesclepius, with an underground ambulatory where religious instruction was conducted.

The hospital in the background, originally a round, two-storey building, was where the famous physician Galen practised in the 2nd century AD.

The former basilica at Pergamum, now known as Kızıl Avlu (the red court) because of its red-brick walls, is located in the centre of the modern town. A monumental, massive building, it was enlarged in the reign of Hadrian (117-138) on the bed of the Selinos River, and was probably devoted to the cult of Serapis. The building was converted in the Byzantine era into a church dedicated to St. John; its right-hand tower now serves as a mosque.

The acropolis is the heart of the ancient site of Pergamum. In the background is the temple of Trajan, built by his adopted son and successor Hadrian over imposing vaulted substrata and surrounded by porticos on three sides. The theatre in the foreground, built into the steep hillside, is impressive for its acoustics and its dimensions (eighty tiered rows seating 10,000 people).

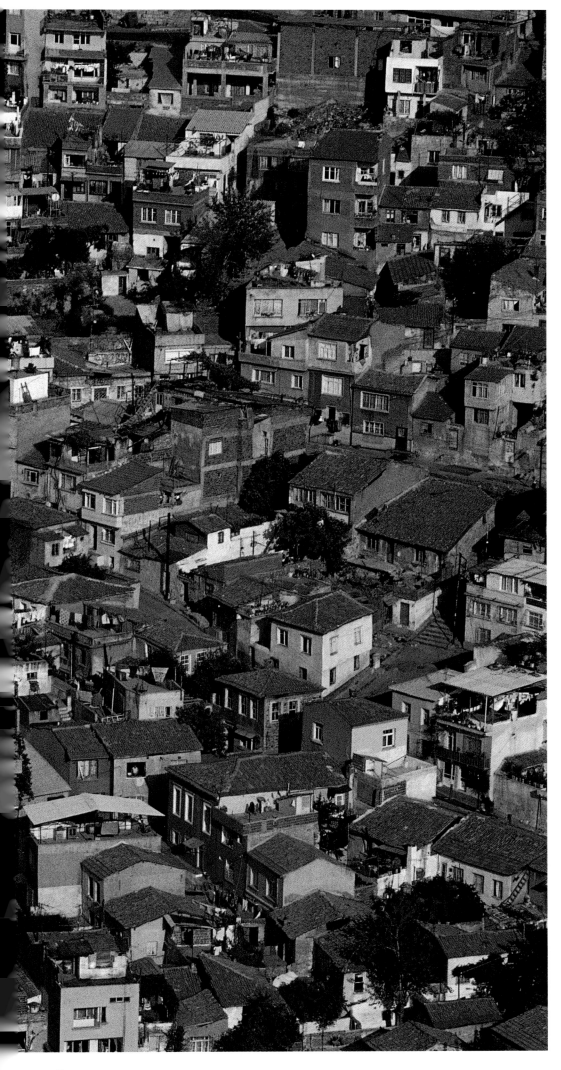

An Izmir neighbourhood that might be in any Turkish city, except for the number of inhabited terraces and blue and ochre colours indicating the proximity of the Aegean. Typical urban domestic architecture was originally of stone; an example is the house on the lower left with its wooden balcony above the door. This style changed with the arrival of reinforced concrete and a greater use of brick. Nonetheless, the neighbourhood has preserved its low houses and some greenery, and – thanks to its sloping site – has remained decidedly resistant to cars, thus maintaining its special charm.

The Antalya livestock market, a disorderly collection of animals, people and trucks. The animals painted red are destined to be sacrificed at a festival. Stands selling food lean against the fence and seed merchants wait for customers. Everyone is going about their business except for one child waving to the photographer in the helicopter.

A tractor's dance of death around the last traces of an ancient culture. With the exception of the eastern regions, the mechanization of agriculture has become increasingly prevalent in a country that is now largely self-sufficient in food production.

The Byzantine citadel of Ephesus, the most important city in Asia Minor during the Greek, Hellenistic, and Roman eras. Silting from the Cayster River (Küçük Menderes) caused the sea to recede, and this ultimately brought about the decline of the city during the Byzantine era. Nonetheless, it was the centre of a Turkic emirate in the 14th and 15th centuries. The ruined mosque in the centre of the citadel dates from this period.

The ruins of the Basilica of St. John the Apostle, built next to the Byzantine citadel in 550 by Justinian. It gave its name to Byzantine Ephesus, called Aghios Theologos, which the Turks in turn called Ayatholuq, or Ayasoluk, before the city was renamed Selçuk in modern times. Behind it is the Isa Beya Mosque built in 1375 by a Damascene architect for a Turkic prince whose name it bears.

The ruins of Roman and Byzantine constructions near the port at Ephesus. The city, seat of the governor of the Roman province of Asia, may have had as many as 250,000 inhabitants under Hadrian. Austrian archaeologists, who have been excavating here for over a hundred years, are still far from having explored all the substrata of the deserted city.

The library built by Tiberius Julius Celsus in AD 135 – its façade restored thanks to funding from the Austrian government – stands at the intersection of Curetes Street as it descends from Magnesia Gate and the sacred way leading to the right towards the theatre. At the bottom of the steps on the right, Mithridates Gate gives onto the agora and what remains of its portico. At the corner made by the two streets lies the brothel with its baths and public latrines.

The Odeum, a small 1,400-seat theatre, built c. AD 150 near the Magnesia Gate, was also used as a meeting place for the aristocracy. To its left, the double temple erected by Augustus and dedicated to Julius Caesar and to Rome. Further to the left, the Prytaneum, the city's government building. In front, the road connecting Magnesia Gate to Curetes Street.

The fate of the port of Miletus was the same as that of its rival Ephesus. Located at the end of a promontory with a harbour that could hold up to two hundred ships, today it lies 8 kilometres (4.5 miles) inland due to alluvial deposits from the Maeander (Büyük Menderes). The site today is less imposing than that of Ephesus and excavations here are not as advanced. Its theatre was one of the most monumental in the ancient world, however.

The Temple of Apollo at Didyma, begun in 332 BC to house an oracle, was one of the largest temples in the ancient world. A dipteros (with double rows of columns) in the Ionian style, it had a total of a 120 columns, most of them 19.7 metres (60 ft.) high and nearly 2 metres (6 ft.) in diameter, though some were never finished. The columns surrounded the cella, which measured 54 x 22 metres (177 x 72 ft.) and was open to the sky because its area was too large to roof.

Bodrum, the site of ancient Halicarnassus, birthplace of Herodotus. The fortress was begun in 1402 by the Knights of St. John, rebuilt in 1480, and handed over to the Turks after the conquest of Rhodes and the expulsion of the Knights in 1523. The town's whitewashed houses with flat roofs are reminiscent of the architecture of the Cyclades.

There are probably more pleasure boats moored in Bodrum today than there were ships at the time of the Knights. This very European resort, the Saint Tropez of the Anatolian coast, welcomes visitors all year round. The brilliantly blue sea, the imposing castle and an abundance of taverns add to its appeal.

The Martyrion of St. Philip at Hierapolis. Christian pilgrims have succeeded the curious of Roman times in visiting the tomb of the apostle who was martyred here in AD 87. The square building had a domed, octagonal chamber within; its sides measured 20 metres (63 ft.) externally. A dome with a wooded framework, dating from the 5th century, covered the central room.

Hierapolis was one of the most famous spas in the Roman province of Asia, possessing a large number of facilities, including a large theatre built under Septimius Severus. This theatre is remarkably well preserved and performances are still given on its restored stage.

The village of Kaleköy with its medieval Turkish fortress built over the ruins of the ancient site of Simena opposite the island of Kekova. PRECEDING PAGES: The white rocks at Hierapolis, called Pamukkale (cotton castle) in Turkish, are a unique geological phenomenon formed from calcareous deposits built up over centuries by mineral-rich water that spouts up from the ground at a temperature of 35°C (95°F) before flowing down the rocks to the plains below.

The island
of Kekova, just off the
coast. During the
Middle Ages, sailors
and pilgrims on their
way to Jerusalem
passed Kekova when
navigating between
Rhodes and Cyprus.
They believed that
divine wrath at the
incestuous affairs of
the Island's Prince had
caused this site to be
flooded in antiquity.
In fact, the flooding
occurred much later.
The foundations of
early buildings can
be seen in outline
under the water, while
ancient Lycian
sarcophagi still
project above.

The fortress at Marmaris, built by Süleyman the Magnificent during the siege of Rhodes in 1522, was surrounded by a small hamlet, traces of which can be seen behind its walls. In the space of two or three decades the town has developed into a flourishing seaside resort, the centre of a network of holiday villages and tourist sites in the surrounding area.

A port of call on the popular "blue cruise", visiting rugged bays and inlets along the Carian, Lycian and Pamphylian coasts, which offers tourists a chance to view both natural beauty and ancient ruins.

Dalyan's
attractions include
Carian and Lycian
ruins at nearby
Caunos; the breeding
ground of the last
sea-turtles in the
Mediterranean; kefal,
a tasty local fish
(like mullet) that
is recommended
in all the guidebooks;
and sandy beaches
scattered with beach
umbrellas and
thatched-roof huts.

Lycian rock
tombs carved in the
cliff-face at Caunos.
PRECEDING PAGES:
A flotilla of boats
taking tourists on an
excursion to the
mouth of Lake
Köyceğiz on their
way to the ancient site
of Caunos near
Dalyan beach.

The size of the theatre at Caunos shows that it was a town of modest aspirations. Many ancient theatres were excessively large owing to the zeal of benefactors who used such extravagant expenditures to help them get elected to public office.

Fethiye, the site of ancient Telmessus, formerly known as Makri, a Greek town abandoned in 1922 and razed by earthquakes in 1950 and 1957. The modern town is a tourist centre with a seafront promenade, but it also possesses ancient sites, including funerary cave temples.

The formidable pirates who were fiinally subdued by Pompey in the 1st century BC had their lairs on the Pamphylian coast. One of these was Phaselis, which combines a picturesque, isolated location with substantial ancient remains, including a theatre, agora and thermal baths, that still attract visitors.

The orientation of Antalya's old city towards the port, now a marina, led to its older dwellings being restored and turned into boarding houses, while bars and restaurants were opened on the waterfront. Services catering for tourists were thus introduced without destroying the character of the city. In the foreground next to the clock tower is Tekeli Mehmet Paşa's mosque, which dates from the 18th century.

Antalya, known as Attaleia in ancient times, was established as a naval base by Attalus II of Pergamum (159-136 BC) and gradually supplanted its neighbour Perge, but it has only ranked as a regional centre since the Seljuk Turkish era. Above, Hadrian's Gate dating from the Roman era. On the right, the old quarter within the city walls, quite well preserved, with its traditional houses surrounded by greenery.

The Seljuk Turk state established in central Anatolia at the end of the 11th century broke out of its isolation by occupying Antalya and the surrounding region at the beginning of the 13th century. The "fluted minaret" (Yivli Minare), which became the symbol of the city, was built by the Seljuk sultan Alaeddin Kaykubad in 1230 as an addition to a mosque converted from a Byzantine church. The latter was destroyed in the following century and replaced by a new mosque built in 1373 by Mübarizüddin Mehmet Bey, ruler of the Turkic emirate of Antalya that succeeded the Seljuks.

A partial view of Antalya's old city. In the middle, the ruined Korkut mosque (the original 5th-century church dedicated to the Virgin was converted to a mosque by Korkut, son of Beyazıt II, at the beginning of the 16th century and burned down in 1851.

Aspendos possessed one of the most beautiful theatres in the ancient world; today this theatre is certainly among the best preserved – in particular its Roman stage plan. Built by a local architect during the reign of Marcus Aurelius (161-180), it is believed to have been transformed into a palace by the Seljuk sultan Alaeddin Kaykubad I (1220-37).

Perge was a Greek city that flourished under the Pax Romana, like most cities in Asia Minor. Most of its monuments therefore date from the Roman or Byzantine periods. In the foreground, the agora with a circular temple in the middle. Behind it, the Hellenistic arch flanked by two towers and preceded by a horseshoe-shaped courtyard. Behind that, the thermal baths with the palæstra in front.

Ruins and cultivated land. Although the presence of ancient sites limits the amount of land which can be cultivated, villages benefit from the spin-off from tourism, as well as from income sent by those who have emigrated to the cities or emigrated to Europe.

Like most of Turkey's ancient sites, Side, an important trading port in the kingdom of Pergamum during the late Hellenistic period, was abandoned at the end of the Byzantine era; it was not resettled until 1898, with the arrival of Turkish refugees from the island of Crete.

Side's archaeological sites and its seaside resort, although complementary elements of the town's attraction for tourists, are located so close to each other that the ancient sites are occasionally threatened by beach-loving visitors. Here, the partially restored temple of Apollo and, to the right of it, the temple of Athena. In the foreground, a Byzantine basilica.

Alanya, called both "Crow's Nest" (Coracesium) and "Beautiful Mountain" (Kalon Oros), was first a pirate's lair and then a naval base during the period of Seljuk rule in Anatolia; a citadel and a shipyard were built here at that time.

The arduous climb required to reach Alanya's citadel has probably saved it from being invaded by the many tourists who prefer to enjoy the beach facilities below, leaving the top of the cliff peaceful and quiet.

Anamur lies at the extreme southern tip of Anatolia, and even banana plantations can be found along the coast. This strategically located but rather unwelcoming part of Rough Cilicia, a pirate's haven, was coveted by the Crusaders, who built an enormous citadel here. The citadel was alternately controlled by the Armenian realm of Cilicia and by the kings of Cyprus. Later, it was taken over by the Seljuks, the Karaman Turkic emirate, and finally the Ottomans.

Traces of the
Crusaders begin in
Anamur. The Crusader
States controlled the
coast from Gaza to
Anamur, and the
Armenian realm
of Cilicia, which held
these lands until 1375,
was part of them.
Among the
fortifications built at
this time were two
castles – one on land,
one on a nearby
island – at Korykos.
The relative isolation
of the latter gave rise
to the legend that a
king had locked up his
daughter here to save
her from a cruel fate,
but of course fate
found her anyway.
Because of thislegend,
the castle is known
locally as Kızkalesi,
or "maiden's tower".

From horizon to horizon run; The foaming violet waves, one after another; The Caspian speaks the child wind's tongue, Speaks and boils over. Who has said, *chort vazmi!* Like a lake that is dead is the Caspian Sea, Unbridled, salt, without end, without home; … (*The Caspian Sea* by Nazim Hikmet.)

When Turkey's nationalist government decided to make Ankara the country's new capital in 1923, their choice was governed by the fact that Ankara, on the Anatolian plateau, was located in the heart of the new nation of Turkey, just as Constantinople (Istanbul) had been the centre of an empire that stretched from the Balkans to the Middle East. Of the ruling powers that have occupied Anatolia during the past 5,000 years, few have confined their domination to Anatolia, but have extended their domains to nearby regions. The truly Anatolian states are considered to be three: the Hittite kingdom of the second millennium BC, the Seljuk kingdom of Anatolia that ruled from the 11th to the 13th centuries, and the Turkish Republic that has existed since 1923, which considers itself the heir to the earlier two, no matter how far removed in time they may be.

The eastern and southern borders of Anatolia have never been easy to define, especially as these areas were inhabited in the past - and in some cases are still inhabited - by non-Anatolian peoples: Armenians in the east and Kurds in the south-east. Anatolia has always possessed a well-defined centre, however, in the Anatolian plateau, at an altitude of 1,000 metres (3,250 ft.). The Pontic range runs along its northern border and separates it from the Black Sea, while the Taurus range runs along its southern edge, defining its Mediterranean border. The western part of Anatolia is characterized by valleys that lead to the Aegean and the Sea of Marmara. To the east, the plateau narrows, wedged between the continuing Pontic range and the Taurus, which form an arc. The plateau rises to 2,000 metres (6,500 ft.) as it reaches the high Euphrates valleys. Beyond the Taurus is Upper Mesopotamia. Two rivers cross the plateau. In the east, the Kızılırmak (Red River), called the Alys in ancient times, forms a large arc whose southernmost point is Avanos in Cappadocia, and then flows northward to reach the Black Sea through a gap in the Pontic range. In the west, the Sabarya, after being diverted to the east, flows into the plains through a gorge down which the Ankara-Istanbul railway line now runs, and then into the Black Sea. Small streams from the surrounding mountains flow into the basin as well; its centre is the Great Salt Lake (Tuz Gölü).

The whole of the plateau can be divided into two parts. One part, north of the Eskişehir-Ankara-Sivas line, is at a higher altitude and has greater annual rainfall as a result of the clouds crossing the Pontic range. The former Hittite capital of Hattusas (today called Boğazköy) is to be found in this region. The area south of this line is more arid, sometimes almost desert-like, and was once referred to as a salt desert. Today, irrigation has reached large portions of these regions, transforming them into the country's breadbasket. Konya, the Seljuk capital, is the centre of this new agricultural activity. Because of the harshness of the plateau's natural

Tents of shepherds during transhumance. In spite of increasing use of new materials, the tents have preserved the forms and structure of traditional Turkic yurts.
PRECEDING PAGES: Nature, history and the everyday life of human beings have been felicitously brought together here in the astonishing landscape of Cappadocia.

A village near Diyarbakır in south-eastern Turkey. There is no trace of modernization here - no pitched roofs, no concrete, no asphalt. Earth is the only building material used.

The island of Akhtamar in Lake Van, residence of Gagik Ardzrouni (908-936), sovereign of Vaspurakan Armenia. The church of the Holy Cross completed in 921 is famous for its decorative relief depicting Old Testament themes.

conditions, cities were usually established along its edges near the foothills of the surrounding mountains, where there were sources of water in mountain torrents that had not yet been absorbed by the dry steppes. An ancient pilgrim route from Istanbul up to the extreme north-west corner of the plateau passed through the cities of Kütahya and Afyon (respectively the capitals of Turkic emirates in the 14th and 15th centuries and rich in Ottoman monuments and traditional houses) and ended at Konya. A railway line from Baghdad built in the 19th century as well as a modern highway both follow this ancient route. While Konya has preserved most of its religious monuments from the Seljuk era and is still the centre of the Mevlevi brotherhood (popularly known as whirling dervishes), Konya has, in this century, lost most of its traditional charm to chaotic urban development.

Beyond Konya, the pilgrim route crossed the Taurus pass and ended at Adana. A branch route leading east and upwards along the edge of the plateau was the main Seljuk and Ottoman military road, and the most important Seljuk monuments lie along this route between Konya and Sivas via Niğde and Kayseri. Urbanization has destroyed the tranquillity of these cities, which were once oases in a desert-like plateau, filled with irrigated gardens, colourful neighbourhoods and impressive monuments. The gardens now contain advertisements, and the monuments are encircled by modern office buildings.

To avoid this long eastern route, which was used mainly by armies to transport supplies, caravans usually took a northern route which ran along the Pontic range. The Istanbul-Ankara highway now follows the westernmost part of this route, which passes mainly through sparsely-populated regions until it reaches a rift in the Pontic range through which the Kızılırmak and Yeşilırmak rivers flow. Here, the abundance of water and of rain-bearing winds from the Black Sea led to the development of prosperous cities: Merzifon, Tokat, and especially Amasya, the city with the greatest number of Ottoman monuments in Anatolia after Bursa. Amasya was the capital of the Hellenistic Pontic kingdom, and the rock tombs of its kings are carved into the boulders which tower over the city. Amasya also possesses Seljuk monuments and numerous old houses. The cities in this region, generally still rather isolated, have managed to keep much of their traditional charm intact.

The two routes join again beyond Sivas near Erzurum, and then continue on to the Iranian border. Between these two main routes, caravan trails crossed the Anatolian plateau diagonally on their way to Bursa via Ankara, or, in later periods, to Izmir. The cities on these roads were not only stops for the caravans but also production centres capable of fueling large-scale regional and even international trade. One example is Tokat, which was a centre for silk-making on the silk road between Tabriz and Bursa and gradually began to specialize in copper utensils when the silk trade declined.

Ankara, located in the heart of a region where angora goats are raised, became the world capital of mohair. The infiltration of manufactured goods from the West during this century has gradually succeeded in destroying most local production in this region, unfortunate timing for local industry which thus lost its chance to exploit the growing tourist trade. In spite of its past, Ankara does not owe its current population of more than two and a half million to its production of wool, but rather to its having been chosen as capital of the new Turkish Republic. It was a city with barely 20,000 inhabitants and the last stop on a railway line in 1920 when the Turkish nationalist movement chose to base itself here; Turkey's parliament, fleeing Allied forces that were occupying Istanbul, moved to Ankara in April of the same year. Ankara was soon virtually rebuilt as a planned urban centre. Hermann Jansen, a German architect who won a 1929 urban-planning contest to devise the future form the city would take, created a system of zoning laws that separated different kinds of activities in the city (a feature popular among urban planners of the day). Thanks to this project, most of which was actually carried out, Ankara seems relatively orderly compared with other Turkish cities. Despite the fact that its population has increased by a factor of 125 since the beginning of this century, Ankara has almost completely preserved its old city centre. Another survivor is the city's famous farmers' market, with its multi-coloured fabrics and spices, and its beautiful wooden mosques from the Seljuk period.

Urban planning unfortunately failed to solve Ankara's housing problems, however, and by the end of the 1930s the first shanty towns appeared - even before Istanbul's - on the hills behind the city. Since that time they have multiplied, and now range all along the city's northern and eastern edges. Some of the oldest shanty towns have preserved the appearance of large villages, even half a century after they were established. The capital, the epitome of an administrative town, employs a labour force drawn from these shanty towns in subordinate administrative jobs at very low salaries, undoubtedly exacerbating the problem. Ankara is also plagued by the extreme climate of the central plateau, with scorchingly hot summers and bitterly cold winters.

In sharp contrast to the central plateau is Turkey's Black Sea coast north of the Pontic range. This coastline, very different from the Aegean coast, is extremely mountainous, rising towards the east. Although its eastern portions receive heavy rainfall, its climate is generally stable. Enough tea is grown in this region to provide for Turkey's domestic consumption, which is very high, as well as to add to the country's exports. To the west of the tea plantations, around Samsun, there are many hazelnut groves as well as tobacco plantations. Corn, introduced in the 18th century, has gradually replaced wheat in this area. Because of the limited amount of agricultural land available between the mountains and the sea, emigration to the large coastal cities of Trabzon and Samsun as

The Taurus Mountains, a region where transhumance is still practised and the last Turkic nomads (yörük) are still to be found.

Hermits of all kinds have always had a penchant for grandiose landscapes, and the persecuted have preferred troglodyte dwellings. A prime example is Cappadocia: here for thousands of years, the hand of man has added to the already extravagant creations of nature by sculpting walls out of rock, hollowing out cones of soft volcanic rock, painting the interiors of caves, and cultivating tiny fields and miniature gardens. The village of Avcılar, in the Göreme valley, is an oasis of square forms in the midst of conical "fairy chimneys".

well as to Istanbul and Ankara has been considerable since the 19th century. This is the first region in modern Turkey, which has a high growth rate, to report a decline in population.

Towards Turkey's eastern border, the landscape becomes less densely populated where the central plateau begins. This area has a harsh climate with temperatures regularly falling below -30°C (-23°F) in winter; it is poor and the rate of emigration is consequently very high. Its landscapes are breathtaking despite - or perhaps because of - their harshness, and some cities in this area contain unimagined treasures. Erzurum is one example, with its many Seljuk monuments. Another is Divriği, with its amazing mosque, which was built during the era of the Mengücek Turkic emirate (by a people who were contemporaries of the Seljuks) and is included on UNESCO's list of World Heritage sites. Further east can be found traces of other cultures: Georgian monasteries near Artvin, the Armenian capital of Ani along the Armenian border, Armenian churches and monasteries around Lake Van and on the island of Akhtamar at the southern end of the lake, and Kurdish castles and fortresses at Doğubeyazıt and Hoşap.

South of the Taurus arc lies Upper Mesopotamia, a steppe that is now being irrigated through the enormous South-east Anatolia Project (GAP), which includes a huge dam on the Euphrates inaugurated in the summer of 1992. An area boasting a very ancient civilization, Upper Mesopotamia has always led a unique existence on the edges of great empires. After Alexander the Great's passage, local kingdoms resisted the Romans for a long time. These included Osroene, an Armenian kingdom whose capital was Edessa (today Urfa), whose kings converted to Christianity at the beginning of the 3rd century; the Adiabene kingdom in the mountains of Kurdistan; and the Commagene kingdom, one of whose rulers, Antiochus I, had a huge monument erected on top of Mount Nemrut Dağ to immortalize his own name. When the Caliphate of Baghdad began to decline, these regions were controlled by Arab chieftains, the Marwanides, based in Diyarbakır, and by Turks, the Artukides, based in Mardin. There was even a free zone set up by Baudouin de Boulogne at Urfa in 1098. From the 16th century to the 19th century, the Kurdish principalities flourished as buffer states between the Ottoman and Persian Empires. Although rural exodus during this

Cappadocia, volcanic formations sculpted over time by erosion, became the refuge of people fleeing invasions or religious persecution. They carved out of the rock churches, monasteries, and enormous underground cities that included cave dwellings. In short, they created an earthly paradise out of a lunar landscape.

century has caused rapid growth of the region's cities - Mardin, Urfa, and Diyarbakır - they have preserved many monuments from their past as well as an unusual style of stone domestic architecture.

Turkey's astonishing variety - its coastlines, its central plain, its modern urban developments, its historic past and the great expanse of teeming life that Istanbul has become - are all revealed when it is seen from the air. Also evident is the country's progress towards Westernization, which has not been without its costs.

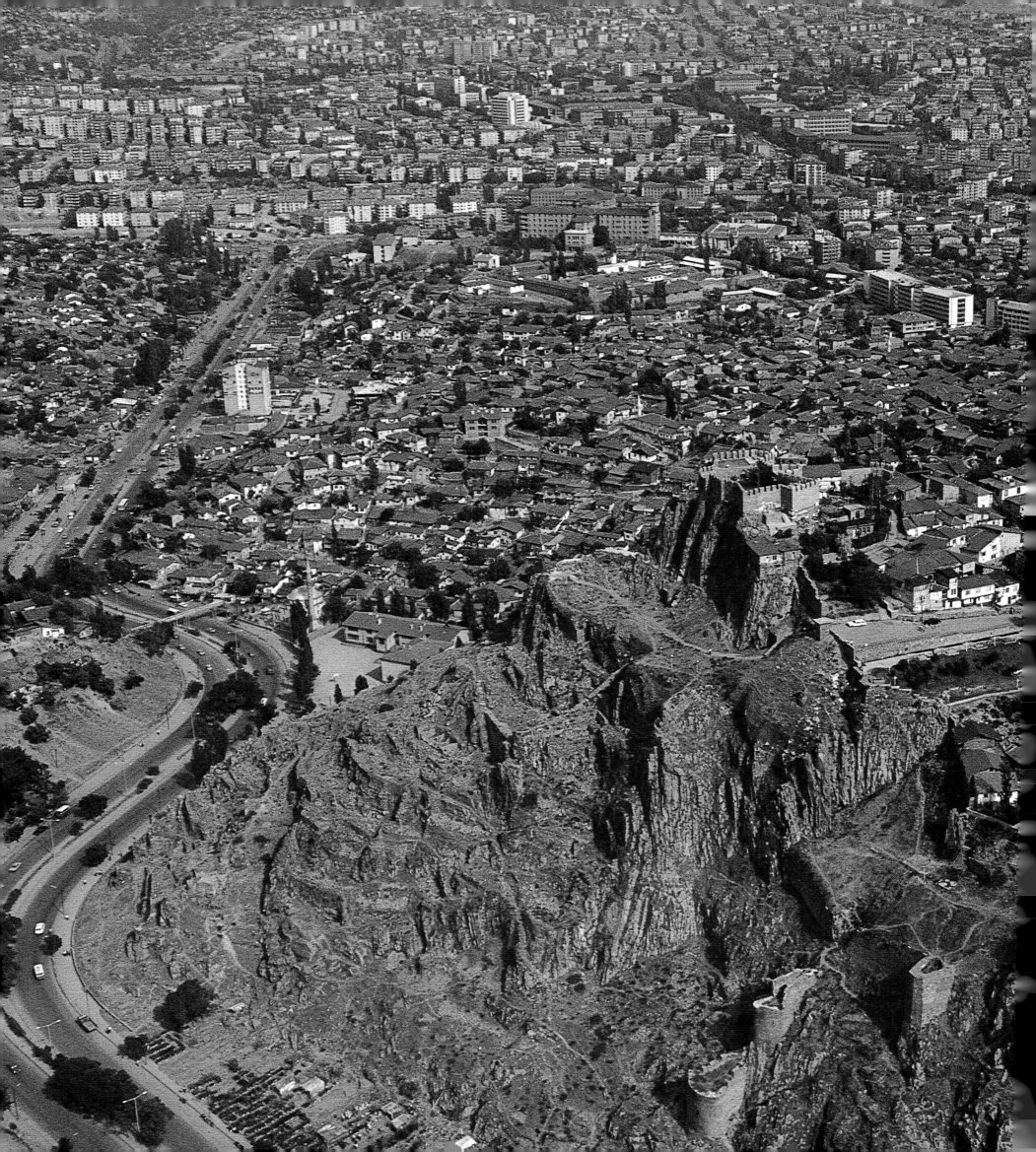

Although the urban explosion in Turkey has often destroyed the traditional character of ancient city centres, Istanbul included, the modern capital, Ankara, has managed to preserve its ancient heart. In the foreground, the town dating from before 1920 is seen enclosed within its citadel. Behind it is the new part of the city and beyond that are the housing estates and shanty towns that all combine to house Ankara's population totalling more than 2.5 million.

The triumphal march of progress destroying the vestiges of the past, is the theme this photograph seems to represent. The buildings on the left are squeezing the first row of houses in a vice-like grip. Not far away, others, huddle together, awaiting a similar fate.

The bedesten (covered market) and caravanserai built below the citadel of Ankara in 1460 by the Grand Vizier Mahmut Paşa. The buildings, in a state of ruin at the beginning of the 20th century, have been restored and today house the Museum of Anatolian Civilizations.

The mausoleum of the founder of the Turkish Republic, Mustafa Kemal Atatürk. Built in a theoretically Neo-Hittite style in order to stress the permanence of Anatolian culture, it is the symbolic Mecca of the capital and the equivalent of the tomb of the unknown soldier. A formal visit by all important official guests is therefore a must.

This mosque that appears faithful to the classic model is a deceptive image: no one climbs up the minarets because the call to prayer is made through a loudspeaker; the half-dome and lateral domes are built of reinforced concrete; and no imperial ceremonies take place in the courtyard. Like a model set down in front of a row of real buildings, the new Ankara mosque is in many ways a hollow representation of past splendour.

Shanty towns are an integral part of large Turkish cities. In Istanbul more substantial tall buildings often replace them and their residents are forced to move to other shanty towns further out. In Ankara, however, where shanty towns have been in existence since the 1930s, they form real villages only a stone's throw from the modern city.

In this well-drained ground, abundantly watered by spring rains but dry in summer, the Christians living in Cappadocia up to 1922 cultivated vineyards that produced a respectable white wine. A winery in Ürgüp, the main town in the region, has continued the tradition, though the grapes used are no longer always grown locally. ABOVE: Turkey's best-known example of a rock city is Zelve, hidden at the end of a small valley and inhabited from the beginning of the Christian era until 1950, when falling rocks caused the last inhabitants to flee.

The architecture of Cappadocia, as seen in the villlage of Göreme, with its flat-roofed masonry cubes pierced by large arches, is far closer in style to that of Upper Mesopotamia and Northern Syria than to that of the rest of Turkey, where wooden structures predominate. Masonry-built houses here were often extended by cave, or troglodyte, dwellings carved out of volcanic cones until public authorities in the 1950s and 1960s, fearing that these structures would collapse, urged their inhabitants to move to new neighbourhoods nearby. Later, proliferation of modern housing devoid of character and the loss of traditional dwellings led the planning authorities to advocate a return to the original houses, in which the troglodyte structures were reinforced.

Troglodyte complexes sometimes develop into whole neighbourhoods or villages, either concealed underground or with openings in the sheer rock face. Dwellings, public areas, places of worship, tombs, stables and eating areas are intermingled, all carved out of the soft rock.

The citadel of Niğde, in central Anatolia, after being drastically "improved" by an overzealous town council. Fortunately, a few flat-roofed houses are still standing around the Seljuk mosque built under Alaeddin Kaykubad I in 1223. The long building in the foreground on the right is a bedesten, or covered market lined with shops.

Divriği, a remote town south-east of Sivas, is famous for its mosque/hospital complex commissioned in 1228 by Ahmet Şah, a ruler of the Mengücek emirate. The building is especially noted for the decorative profusion of the floral-motif bas reliefs on its façade, and has been designated a World Heritage site by UNESCO.

A typical village on the Anatolian plateau, located on a hillside at the end of the only road leading to it. The mosque, built above shops at ground-floor level, is probably a recent addition. Newly built houses extending the village can be seen on either side of the road, while a few houses in traditional style still remain in the background.

The salt lake,
whose outline changes
according to variations
in rainfall, occupies
the heart of the salt
desert on the central
Anatolian plateau.
With increased use of
irrigation for agriculture
despite the formidable
problems presented
by its salinity, the lake
is in the process of
shrinking and will soon
dry up completely.

The houses in this village seem to have been built haphazardly, but in fact the purpose is to leave each a private space partly enclosed by a wall. Houses built in the traditional way, such as the one in the left foreground, are gradually giving way to those constructed with mortar, pitched roofs and bricks.

A mountain village, clinging to an arid hillside without the slightest vegetation, precisely follows the terraced contours of the land. Houses are built in clay and straw with sod roofs. The long buildings serve as both dwellings and barns while a fewpoles indicate the availability of electricity, no road system is visible. The village's mosque with its blue roof is the only real sign of modernization.

A sheep farm on the high plateau, where modern buildings, with their mass-produced tiles and concrete terraces, are combined with pens whose form and structure date back to Neolithic times. The vast distances between hamlets in the eastern part of the country make constructing a road network here both difficult and costly; this remains one of the major obstacles in efforts to modernize Turkey's outlying areas.

In spite of the regular forms of the fields and furrows, this farmland has not yet been completely tamed. There are still trees and groves to provide shade for workers during meals or siestas. In spite of the increase in single-crop farming, which mechanization has made profitable – wheat in the Konya region, cotton on the Cilician plain (Çukurova), and sunflowers in Thrace – many small farmers have resisted this trend and plant various crops on their land.

Women in the fields and men in the towns - a traditional division of labour, although the men are called on to help with more arduous farm tasks such as planting and harvesting.
FOLLOWING PAGES:

Birecik on the Euphrates where caravans from Aleppo once loaded their bundles onto large circular rafts on which they were transported downstream to Fallujah, not far from Baghdad.

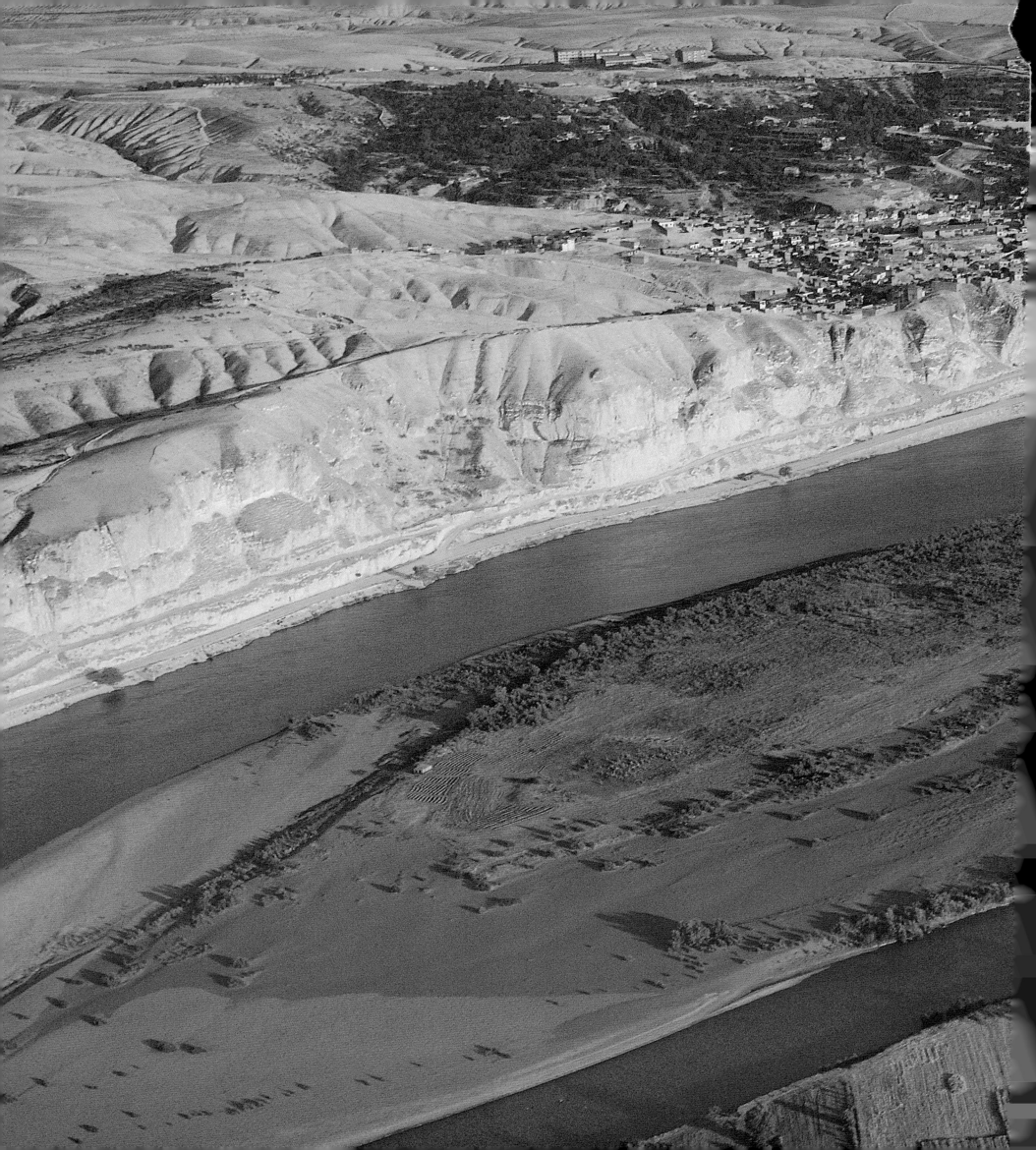

Nemrut Dağ is the grandiose folly of a Hellenistic king, Antiochus I Commagene (62-34 BC), who decided to immortalize himself by having a crushed stone burial mound – 150 metres in diameter and 50 metres high (489 ft. by 163 ft.) – built on top of a 2,000 metre (6,600 ft.) mountain. The mound is flanked by two terraces facing east and west, and decorated with colossal statues representing the king surrounded by Greek and Iranian gods.

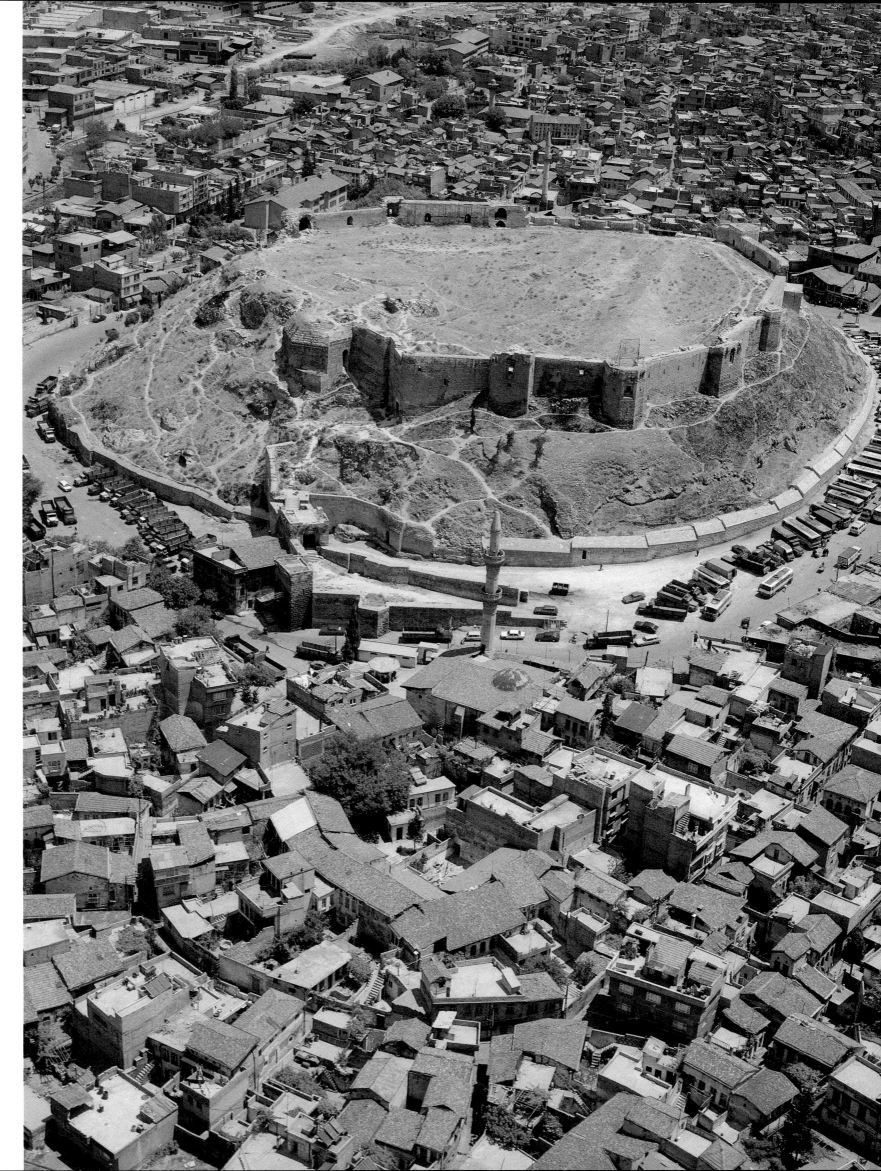

The cities of Gaziantep in Turkey and Aleppo in Syria both have pistachio groves and a citadel built on top of a hill. Built by Justinian, the citadel in Gaziantep was later rebuilt by the Seljuks. With a population of over 600,000, Gaziantep is the largest city in the south-east of the country and the sixth-largest in Turkey.

Kurdish feudalism in the east gave rise to the building of castles, not found in most other parts of the country. The palace/castle Hoşap Fortress, upstream from Van, was built in 1643 by Sarı Süleyman Bey, a Kurdish chieftain.

A watchtower inland from the port of Trabzon. The city, known under the Byzantine Empire as Trebizond, was conquered by the Turks in 1461. Until the beginning of the 20th century it was inhabited by a mixture of Greek, Armenian, Laze, and Turkic peoples.

The monastery of the Virgin of Sumela, founded in 385 under Theodosius I. Generously subsidized by Alexius Comnenus III of Trebizond (1349-90), it was also protected by Mehmet II the Conqueror. The last monks left in 1923 at the time of the population exchange between Greeks and Turks.

Although ample rainfall in the Black Sea region makes possible the cultivation of hazelnut trees and tea plantations, numerous forested areas limit the size of fields and inhibit large-scale arable farming. Small farms here are often rudimentary. Here, in the Kastamonu area, farm workers are seen using a swing plough drawn by oxen.

An oasis of orchards and gardens in the centre of the Anatolian plateau near Aksaray is a sharp contrast to its arid surroundings. Village dwellings built with clay and straw blend into the landscape.

Built in 1784, the castle of Ishak Paşa, a Kurdish notable, is an astonishingly eclectic construction that combines Baroque details borrowed from the West, with Armenian, Seljuk and Persian influences to produce a castle that seems out of a tale from "A Thousand and One Arabian Nights", the Oriental equivalent of Ludwig II of Bavaria's castle at Neuschwanstein. Mount Ararat is seen in the background; an extinct volcano, it reaches a height of 5,165 metres (16,941 ft.).

Beyond the castle of Ishak Paşa, in an otherworldly landscape just a few miles from the Iranian border, the castle of Doğubeyazıt, with its Urartian foundations dating from before the 8th century BC, was occupied by many successive rulers until the Ottomans took control of it. A mosque was added during the reign of Selim I (1512-20).

INDEX OF PLACES

22	Perge	**29**	Ankara	**36**	Lake Van
23	Aspendos	**30**	Göreme	**37**	Hoşap
24	Side	**31**	Niğde	**38**	Castle of Ishak Paşa
25	Alanya	**32**	Gaziantep	**39**	Doğubeyazıt
26	Anamur	**33**	Birecik	**40**	Mount Ararat
27	Konya	**34**	Nemrut Dağ	**41**	Trabzon
28	Lake Tuz Gölü	**35**	Diyarbakır	**42**	Divriği

TRAVEL AND TOPOGRAPHY

Bean, George. *Aegean Turkey,* London, 1966
Turkey's Southern Shore, London, 1968
Turkey Beyond the Maeander, London, 1971
Lycia, London, 1978

Berry, Burton Y. *Out of the Past: the Istanbul Grand Bazaar,* New York, 1977

Michaud, Roland and Sabrina. *Turkey,* London, 1986

Stark, Freya. *Alexander's Path,* London, 1958; paperback edition, New York, 1984

Stark, Freya, and Roiter, Fulvio. *Turkey,* London, 1971

Williams, Gwyn. *Turkey. A Traveller's Guide and History,* London, 1967
Eastern Turkey. A Guide and History, London, 1972

HISTORY, ANCIENT AND MODERN

Bamm, Peter. *Alexander the Great: Power as Destiny,* London, 1965

Blegen, Carl W. *Troy and the Trojans,* London, 1963

Boardman, John. *The Greeks Overseas. Their Early Colonies and Trade;* paperback edition, London, 1981

Browning, Robert. *Justinian and Theodora,* London, 1987

Ferrill, Arthur. *The Fall of the Roman Empire,* London, 1986; paperback edition 1990

Hotham, David. *The Turks,* London, 1972

Hoyt, Edwin P. *Disaster at the Dardanelles, 1915,* London, 1976

Inalcik, Halil. *The Ottoman Empire,* London, 1973

James, Robert Rhodes. *Gallipoli,* London and New York, 1965

Jenkins, Romilly. *Byzantium. The Imperial Centuries (A.D. 610-1071),* London, 1966

Kinross, Lord. *Atatürk: The Rebirth of a Nation,* London, 1964
The Ottoman Centuries, London and New York, 1977

Lehman, Johannes. *The Hittites: People of a Thousand Gods,* London, 1977

Lewis, Bernard. *The Emergence of Modern Turkey,* Oxford, 1961
Istanbul and the Civilization of the Ottoman Empire, Norman, Oklahoma, 1963

Lloyd, Seton. *Ancient Turkey: a Traveller's History,* London, 1992

Luce, J.V. *Homer and the Homeric Age,* London, 1975

Maclagan, Michael. *The City of Constantinople,* London, 1968

Macqueen, J.G. *The Hittites and their Contemporaries in Asia Minor,* London and Boulder, Colorado, 1975; revised edition, London, 1986

Mansfield, Peter. *The Ottoman Empire and its Successors,* London, 1973

Mellaart, James. *Earliest Civilizations of the Near East,* London, 1965

Runciman, Steven. *Byzantine Civilization, London,* 1933
The Fall of Constantinople, 1453, Cambridge, 1965

Sandars, N.K. *The Sea Peoples: Warriors of the Ancient Mediterranean,* London, 1978

Shaw, Stanford J., and Shaw, Ezal Kural. *History of the Ottoman Empire and Modern Turkey* (2 vols.), Cambridge, 1976, 1977

ART AND ARCHITECTURE

Akurgal, Efrem. *The Art of the Hittites* (with photographs by Max Hirmer), London, 1962
Ancient Civilizations and Ruins of Turkey, Ankara, 1983

Aslanapa, Oktay. *Turkish Art and Architecture,* New York and London, 1971

Atasoy, Nurhan, and Raby, Julian. *Iznik: The Pottery of Ottoman Turkey,* London, 1989

Ford, P. R. J. *The Oriental Carpet: A History and Guide to Traditional Motifs, Patterns, and Symbols,* New York, 1981

Freely, John, and Burelli, Augusto Romano. *Sinan. Architecture of Süleyman the Magnificent and the Ottoman Golden Age,* London, 1992

Goodwin, Godfrey. *A History of Ottoman Architecture,* London 1971, and Baltimore, Maryland, 1980; paperback edition 1992

Levey, Michael. *The World of Ottoman Art,* London and New York, 1975

Mainstone, Rowland J. *Haghia Sophia. Architecture, Structure and Liturgy of Justinian's Great Church,* London, 1988

Onians, John. *Art and Thought in the Hellenistic Age: The Great World View 350-50 BC.* London, 1979

Rodley, Lyn. *Cave Monasteries of Byzantine Cappadocia,* Cambridge, 1986

Scherer, Margaret R. *The Legends of Troy in Art and Literature,* New York and London, 1963

GUIDO ALBERTO ROSSI AND EDITIONS DIDIER MILLET WISH TO THANK
CAPTAIN OMER ORUCOGLU FOR HIS PRECIOUS COLLABORATION.
PHOTOGRAPHY CREDITS:
COLLECTION PIERRE DE GIGORD: PAGES 14/15, 22-23, 24-25
ARA GÜLER: PAGES 17 (MATRAKI MAP IN THE TOPKAPI MUSEUM), 18,
26/27 (AFTER G. BERGGREN), 146, 184-185, 186/187
COLLECTION D.M: PAGE 20
ORHAN DURGUT: PAGES 145, 162/163, 164, 174/175, 176-177, 178/179,
180-181, 182-183

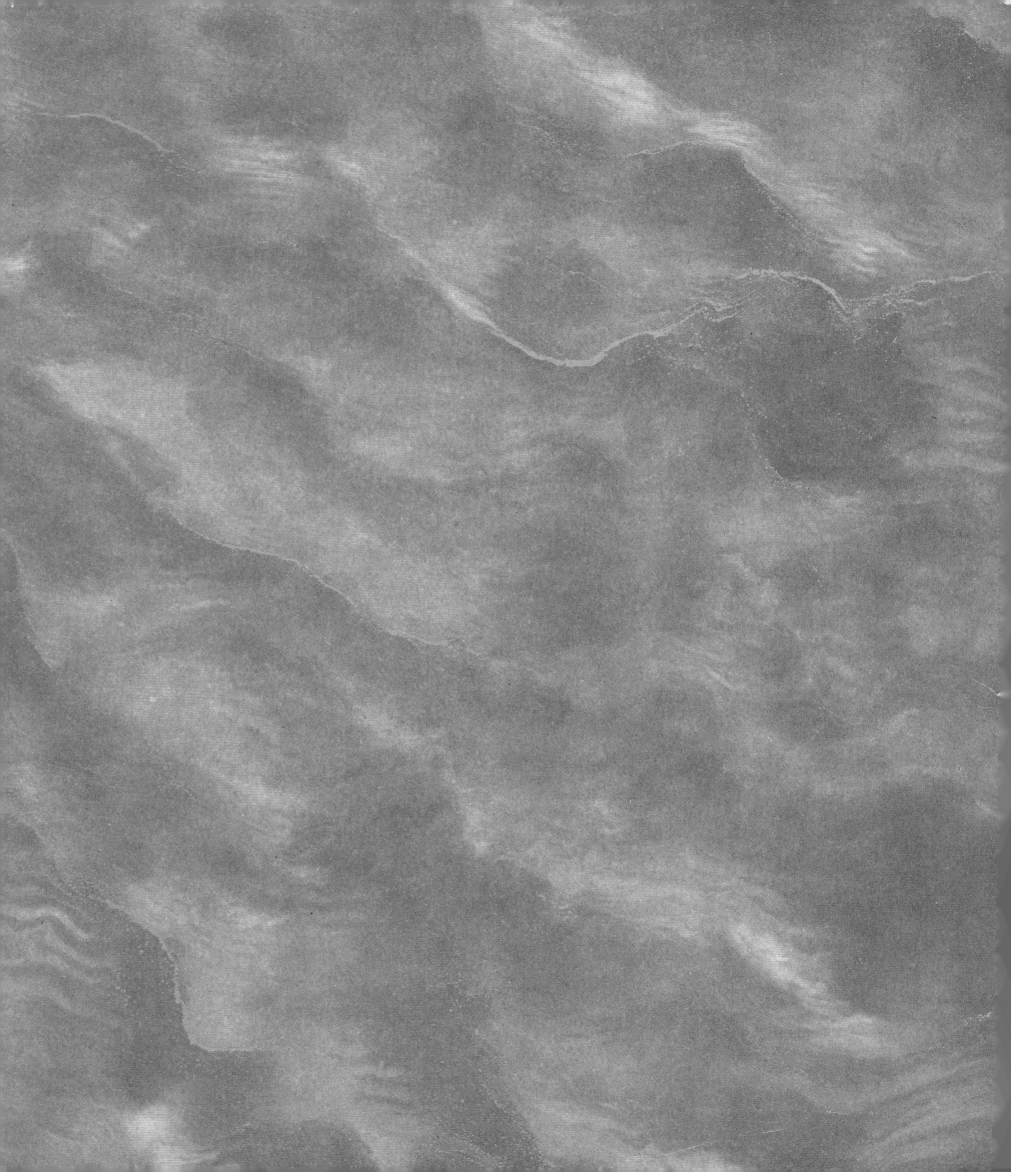